Plea Bargaining or Trial?

Plea Bargaining or Trial?

The Process of Criminal-Case Disposition

Lynn M. Mather
Dartmouth College

Lexington Books
D.C. Heath and Company
Lexington, Massachusetts
Toronto

Library of Congress Cataloging in Publication Data

Mather, Lynn M.
  Plea bargaining or trial?

  Bibliography: p.
  Includes index.
  1. Plea bargaining—California—Los Angeles Co. 2. Criminal justice, Administration of—California—Los Angeles Co. I. Title.
KFC1199.L62C766   345'.79443'072   75-41560
ISBN 0-669-00467-7

Published simultaneously in Canada

Printed in the United States of America

International Standard Book Number: 0-669-00467-7

Library of Congress Catalog Card Number: 75-41560

To my mother and
the memory of my father
Rae and Cecil Moss

Contents

List of Figure
and Tables

Figure

Tables

Acknowledgments

Thanks first go to my husband, Mike Mather, for his perceptive comments on the manuscript, his editorial assistance, and, most of all, his constant encouragement. Even when I wondered if I would ever finish, Mike had no doubts; his faith and patience were indispensable.

I want to thank Laura Nader for inspiring my interest in ethnography and showing me the value of an anthropological approach to the study of law. Her ideas and enthusiasm were essential to this study.

I am especially grateful to Martin M. Shapiro for his valuable advice, strong support, and intellectual guidance throughout this research and writing. His careful reading of several drafts and many constructive suggestions have been greatly appreciated. This book has benefited enormously from his interest and help, and I have learned a great deal from him.

I also want to thank William K. Muir and Lief Carter, who read the manuscript in an earlier version and gave me valuable comments and friendly encouragement. Various sections of the manuscript were read by Marc Galanter, John A. Gardiner, Herbert Jacob, Nelson Kasfir, David Neubauer, and Richard Winters, and I appreciate their comments and criticism. My colleagues at Dartmouth have provided me with a stimulating and supportive environment in which to work, and I am also grateful to the Faculty Research Committee at Dartmouth for their financial support.

I am indebted to the judges, defense attorneys, prosecutors, and court staff of the Los Angeles Superior Court for willingly accepting me into their world and cooperating so generously with my research. Thanks also go the administrative offices of the Los Angeles Superior Court and to the California Bureau of Criminal Statistics for providing me with statistical data.

Some of the material presented here appeared in an earlier form in the *Law and Society Review* (Mather 1974a), *The Potential for Reform of Criminal Justice* (Mather 1974b), and *Public Law and Public Policy* (Mather 1977). I am grateful to the Law and Society Association, Sage Publications, and Praeger Publishers, respectively, for permission to revise and use that material.

1 Introduction

This book describes how criminal cases are settled in a large urban court. In the court—as in most American courts—only a small fraction of the criminal cases are decided by adversary trial; the vast majority are resolved by some form of plea bargaining. This book addresses itself to the question: what determines whether a case is settled by plea bargaining or by trial? In investigating this question, I examine the court process from the perspective of regular court participants; that is, I use some anthropological field methods to describe how courtroom actors evaluate their cases to decide between negotiated or trial dispositions.

There are three goals for this book. The first is to suggest the factors which are most important for determination of a guilty plea or trial case disposition. Other criminal court studies have indicated the importance of variables such as caseload pressures for the prosecutor, strength or weakness of the case, type of defense attorney, personal characteristics of the defendant (age, race, prior record, bail status), or the type of crime involved.[1] What is not clear from the literature, however, is the relative significance of these factors in determining the method of case disposition.[2] Nor is it clear how these factors are weighted when they are seen from different points of view; most of the early studies, in particular, focused on the interests of either the prosecutor, the defense attorney, or the defendant.[3] For example, weakness in the prosecution's case might lead the prosecutor to offer greater concessions toward a guilty plea, and yet that same weakness might incline the defendant and/or his attorney to pursue an adversary trial. In my research, I have tried to encompass the viewpoints of different participants in the courtroom (with the exception of defendants, as explained later in this chapter), as well as to describe the relative importance of these various factors as they lead to a guilty plea or trial disposition.

A second aim is to present an empirical study of the case disposition process in an urban criminal court, with particular attention to the dynamics of plea bargaining. Thus, I describe case disposition in the Los Angeles County Superior Court (Central District). We know that criminal courts vary from one jurisdiction to the next along such issues as: the frequency of guilty pleas; the dominance of the judge or prosecutor over plea negotiations; the stage at which bargaining is likely to occur (for example, complaint filing, preliminary hearing, or trial date); the implicit or explicit nature of the bargaining; and whether the bargaining centers on the charge or on the sentence.[4] In spite of this variation,

1

one might argue for a basic similarity of all criminal court processes given the fact that, in most cases, informal, discretionary decisions predominate over formal legal processes (for example, see Rosett and Cressey 1976:45). Indeed the debate over the pros and cons of plea bargaining seems to assume that the dynamics of the process are by and large the same throughout the United States. But while some conclude that plea bargaining promotes justice, others see the process as corrupt, discriminatory, and full of abuses. Perhaps there are genuine differences in the nature and spirit of plea bargaining in different courts. Good case studies will aid in the normative discussion of plea negotiation as well as providing material for a more general empirical theory of criminal court processes.[5]

In presenting the Los Angeles criminal courts, I will describe a system in which: the majority of defendants pled *not* guilty, but most were then convicted in an abbreviated court trial which operated as a "slow plea" of guilty;[6] the judge, as well as the prosecutor, played an important role in plea bargaining; both implicit and explicit bargaining occurred; there were sentence bargaining and charge bargaining, according to the offense involved; and there was no sentence differential between trial and nontrial dispositions perceived by attorneys for many minor felony offenses.

The third, and perhaps most important, goal of this book is to show the usefulness of ethnography for an understanding of court processes. Ethnography—that is, the description of a culture—is used here to describe the subculture of a criminal court. Attorneys and judges, working daily on the disposition of criminal cases, come to share an understanding of the meaning of different kinds of cases and of the appropriate dispositions for these cases. The participants speak the same language, frequently using legal terms or legal categories to convey information on the social features of cases. These regular courtroom actors also follow a set of informal norms on how to behave with their colleagues, involving, for example, the kinds of information that are appropriately shared, the social significance of certain behaviors, and the implications of various pretrial strategies. We can learn a great deal about the internal dynamics of a criminal court by discovering the native point of view—that is, by understanding how regular court participants organize their reality.

Thus, in investigating the factors associated with a bargained or trial case disposition, I tried to discover those factors which were culturally significant for the courtroom actors. I examined the criteria used by my informants as they defined, interpreted, and described their cases and their experiences. The book discusses these criteria with the aim of showing the insiders' view of the choice between plea bargaining and trial. An important contribution of this ethnographic approach is that it reveals an order and a coherence to the seemingly arbitrary or chaotic informal decision-making. One criticism of plea bargaining is:

Unlike trial—an open system that can be studied, observed, and eventually mastered—plea negotiation is a closed-door process not governed by even a rudimentary set of rules (Alschuler 1975:1270).

To the contrary, the following chapters suggest that, at least in one court system, there *are* rules for the plea bargaining process which can be studied and observed; they are rules embedded in the social and cultural experience of the courtroom.

Although I completed my research before Rosett and Cressey's (1976) book was published, the data presented here nicely illustrate their notion of a "subculture of justice within the courthouse" (1976:91). Rosett and Cressey (1976:90-91) describe this subculture as follows:

> Even in the adversary world of law, men who work together and understand each other eventually develop shared conceptions of what are acceptable, right and just ways of dealing with specific kinds of offenses, suspects and defendants. These conceptions form the bases for understandings, agreements, working arrangements and cooperative attitudes. . . . Over time, these shared patterns of belief develop the coherence of a distinct culture, a style of social expression peculiar to the particular courthouse.

My book describes the subculture of the courthouse in Los Angeles and shows not only the shared attitudes, values, and informal norms of cooperation, but also the limits to those cooperative agreements in cases which are resolved by adversary trial.

The remainder of this chapter discusses the ethnographic approach in greater detail, and then describes the setting and methods for this research study.

Ethnography

The concept of ethnography is basic to cultural anthropology. Essentially, an ethnography is a description of a culture. Conklin (1968:172) defines an ethnographer as "an anthropologist who attempts . . . to record and describe the culturally significant behaviors of a particular society." Ethnography examines how people think about what they do and how they organize and interpret the actions of others. This is what is meant by the task of describing a culture; the task is not simply to describe the customary behaviors, but is also to describe the cultural meaning of those behaviors. As Goodenough suggests:

> Culture is not a material phenomenon; it does not consist of things, people, behavior, or emotions. It is rather an organization of these things. It is the forms of things that people have in mind, their models for perceiving, relating, and otherwise interpreting them (1964:36).

An ethnographic approach to the study of law can be contrasted with a legalistic approach. Where a legalistic perspective views legal processes and decisions in the context of formal legal rules and procedures, an ethnographic perspective sees these processes in the context of informal rules and social interactions of the participants. An ethnographic approach focuses on the network and interactions of persons dealing with "things legal" so that legal ideas, rules, and behaviors are but another aspect of ongoing social life (Nader and Yngvesson 1973).

Viewing law in its social and cultural context leads to: a concern for "folk systems" of justice within a particular society; an interest in disputes, especially trouble cases, and how they are handled; research on the decision-making process within a court system; investigation of the relation between courts and alternative forms of dispute settlement; and a questioning of the social and cultural factors that determine the choice of one method of dispute resolution over another (see, for example, the collection of articles in Nader 1965 and 1969).

Frake (1969a:124) describes two important attributes of ethnography.[7] First, the ethnographer attempts to describe the rules of culturally appropriate behavior rather than to predict actual behavior. Hence:

> The model of an ethnographic statement is not: "if a person is confronted with stimulus X, he will do Y," but: "if a person is in situation X, performance Y will be judged appropriate by native actors" (Frake 1969a:124).

Frake explains this point further in another paper (1969b:471) when he notes that

> a failure of an ethnographic statement to predict correctly does not necessarily imply descriptive inadequacy as long as the members of the described society are as surprised by the failure as is the ethnographer.

A second attribute of ethnography is that "the ethnographer seeks to discover, not prescribe, the significant stimuli in the subject's world" (Frake 1969a:124). This point is of particular importance in ethnographic work. The ethnographer must learn *in the field* the objects and behaviors which are culturally significant for the particular society. In contrast, the survey re-searcher, for example, must define the data he considers to be significant *before* he begins his study.

In order to describe a culture, the researcher must spend considerable time in direct contact with the people he is studying; indeed, the fieldwork experience is essential for ethnographic work. Fieldwork includes a long period of observation and participation in a well-defined community, knowledge of the spoken language, and a greater use of informants than of documentary or survey data (Conklin 1968:172). Sociologists tend to use the term "participant observation" rather than "fieldwork" to encompass this range of observational methods (McCall and Simmons 1969:1).

An ethnographic approach to the study of criminal court processes is particularly useful for understanding case disposition in terms of a negotiation process. The settlement of a criminal case is generally not a situation of pure conflict (a zero-sum game). Instead the process is primarily a bargaining situation or a "mixed-motive" game in which there is some cooperation as well as opposition between the parties. Schelling (1963) pointed out that the outcome of a mixed-motive game, or any bargaining process, may depend upon the dynamics of the social process itself and not simply on a priori data. Hence, data on the social perceptions and interactions of participants are needed to understand the final outcome of the bargaining. This kind of data is most easily obtained by working from an ethnographic perspective.

The Setting

This book describes the disposition process for adult felony cases in the central district of the Superior Court of Los Angeles County. The Los Angeles Superior Court, the largest single trial court in the nation, serves a population of over 7 million in the county. In 1970-71, the period of this research, the Los Angeles Superior Court handled over one-half of the felony cases in California.

Each county in California has one superior court, with original jurisdiction over all matters concerning juveniles, all criminal cases involving felonies (offenses punishable by one year or more in state prison), and all civil cases involving over $5,000. Misdemeanor cases, lesser civil suits, preliminary hearings for felonies, and traffic violations are heard in the municipal courts (for districts with over 40,000 people) or the justice courts (for districts less than 40,000). The County of Los Angeles consists of about seventy-five cities and numerous unincorporated areas. The largest city in the county is Los Angeles, with a population of close to 3 million. The county is governed by a five-member board of supervisors. Board members are selected from five districts in nonpartisan elections.

Los Angeles government, along with its nonpartisan "reformed" politics, is most noted for its extreme decentralization, a decentralization which characterizes both the formal structure of authority and the informal patterns of influence (Banfield and Wilson 1963:110). There are numerous independent government commissions and boards in Los Angeles, each operating in its own sphere, free from centralized supervision. The criminal courts themselves are characterized by relatively autonomous operation of the various municipal courts, the Los Angeles County Superior Court, the district attorney's office (which handles felonies), the various city attorneys' offices (each handling misdemeanors), and the countywide public defender's office. In addition, as Balbus (1973:31-37) suggests, the low cohesion of the political system in Los Angeles is matched by a somewhat weak and disorganized private defense community, at least insofar as the bar is likely to articulate the interests of minority-group defendants. The Los Angeles County Public Defender's Office is generally well respected, with adequate investigative resources and a strong, competent staff of attorneys.

The Superior Court of Los Angeles County is decentralized, with a separate courthouse and caseload for each of its nine geographic districts.[8] I conducted the research for this book in the central district, located in downtown Los Angeles. I chose to study the central district for several reasons. It was the largest of the districts of the superior court, both in caseload and staff. In 1967, about 60 percent of the felony cases in the county were heard in the central district, although by 1971 the proportion had decreased to 37 percent as a result of greater decentralization (Berger 1967; Greenwood and associates 1976). The central district also dealt with the highest concentration of inner-city serious crime. Almost two-fifths of the felonies in Los Angeles County were prosecuted in the central district, while only one-fifth of the county's population lived within the district in 1970 (Villasenor, 1971). Most defendants in the central district were inner-city blacks and Mexican-Americans, in contrast to defendants in outlying districts (or "branch courts") who were more often Anglo-American, middle class and suburban.[9] Also, proportionately more defendants were represented by the public defender in the central district than were defendants in other districts.

At the center of the district is downtown Los Angeles, with its commercial and manufacturing interests, city hall, and other government office buildings. Residential areas in the central district include small ethnic neighborhoods such as Chinatown and Little Tokyo, a number of Mexican-American neighborhoods in East Los Angeles, predominantly black communities south and southwest of downtown, and Griffith Park and older sections of Hollywood to the north.[10]

The criminal division of the central district, which handled the felony cases, was one of several specialized legal divisions (for example, family law, probate, juvenile) of the superior court downtown. A supervising judge presided over each division; in the criminal division the supervising judge sat in a master calendar department and assigned cases to one of twenty-six trial departments. In 1970, these departments were located in three different buildings:[11] the Hall of Justice, the Brunswig Building, and the Old Hall of Records. The Hall of Justice, an impressive old twelve-story building, was the focal point for the criminal courts. The district attorney's offices, the public defender's offices, the superior court records and case files, the master calendar department, and ten superior court trial departments were all located in the Hall of Justice. In addition, the top three floors of the Hall of Justice were county jail facilities holding over 3,000 persons, most of them awaiting trial. Across from the Hall of Justice was the Brunswig Building, a small, older building that used to be a pharmaceutical factory. Ten trial departments were located in the Brunswig Building, and the courtrooms themselves were a shabby contrast to the wood-paneled large rooms in the Hall of Justice. Just down the street, there were six more trial departments in the Old Hall of Records, a thirteen-story Victorian building that was torn down in 1972.

Associated with each of the twenty-six criminal trial departments was a superior court judge, court clerk, reporter, bailiff, and two or three deputy district attorneys who prosecuted all of the cases assigned to that courtroom. Also, the same two or three deputy public defenders generally had settings for cases in one particular courtroom. Every year, in January, these assignments were rotated, with many of the judges, attorneys, and staff moving to other courtrooms. During the year each courtroom took on its own character with the daily interaction of a small group of people. Thus, courtroom workgroups in Los Angeles were relatively stable. This stability did, indeed, as hypothesized by Eisenstein and Jacob (1977:35-38), produce patterns of mutual dependence, familiarity, sharing of information, and plea negotiation.

One distinctive feature of courtroom workgroups in Los Angeles was the ease with which defense attorneys and prosecutors could transfer their cases to two particular courtrooms called "short cause" courts. These courts only handled cases whose dispositions would take less than one hour and would not require a jury. Judges who were known to be lenient in sentencing were usually assigned to the short cause departments which facilitated negotiated dispositions. There was rather high circulation of attorneys from their regular assigned judge to the short cause judges.[12] This circulation encouraged communication among attorneys and cut down on the isolation of each workgroup. Finally, although relations among defense and prosecuting attorneys were friendly and informal within each courtroom, each participant still felt a strong sense of identification and allegiance with his own organization. For example, public defenders and prosecutors did not tend to socialize with each other outside of their courtroom; at the noon recess attorneys went to their respective offices (public defender or district attorney) to meet colleagues for lunch.

Research Methods

Data for this study come from extensive observation, interviews, examination of case files, and the collection of some statistical information. I began my fieldwork in July 1970, observing case dispositions in the central district and informally asking attorneys and others about cases I had observed. Attorneys, judges, and court staff were all very open and receptive to my questions. One problem I had at the beginning was being too closely identified with either the public defender's or the district attorney's office. At first, when a public defender saw me talking with several district attorneys, he assumed that I worked in the district attorney's office. And I also encountered prosecutors who were suspicious of me because they had seen me earlier with a public defender. I dealt with this problem by making a conscious effort to spend equal time with attorneys on both sides, explaining that I was an academic researcher studying the whole criminal court process. I also enlisted the aid of several judges to introduce me to others in court. After a time, I had an identity independent of any one party and I was included in the regular work routine of the court; that is, prosecutors, defense attorneys, and judges let me sit in on their discussions of cases and listen to their "shop talk."

I learned a great deal simply by listening to the participants talk to each other about their cases—about the problems, the strategies, the expectations, and the risks involved in alternative dispositions. I watched cases being settled by brief phone conversations in attorneys' offices, by meetings by attorneys during court recess, and by discussions in judges' chambers. Then I also observed the official, formal proceedings in court which finalized the guilty-plea settlements. I tried to ask the participants why certain settlements were chosen and why others were rejected. At the conclusion of a case, I sometimes went with an attorney to his office, asking him about the specific case disposition and about more general patterns in the court. Once in the office, I heard the attorney talk with his colleagues as they came in to report on their cases, ask advice, complain about certain judges, and so forth.

The informal plea negotiations between prosecuting and defense attorneys usually occurred in the courtrooms, before the sessions began or during one of the frequent recesses. Discussions also took place in the judges' chambers, although discussions with the judges were generally quite brief. Five judges agreed to let me sit in on these sessions in chambers; I observed about twenty hours of discussion in chambers. My research lasted one year, with five months of almost daily observation in superior court and several weeks of observation of felony arraignments and preliminary hearings in municipal court. In addition, I had longer interviews with about eighty participants (judges, defense attorneys, prosecutors, probation officers, and court staff), using open-ended interviews. About one-half of these interviews lasted over an hour, and some for two or three hours. I also examined the case files (which contained the probation reports used in sentencing) on about thirty of the cases I had observed (particularly those settled by trial) and I did some follow-up interviews on those cases. Finally, I gathered some statistical data to test relationships which I had discovered from observations and interviews.

During the course of my fieldwork I did not systematically apportion my time among the twenty-six trial courtrooms, since I was studying the network of people involved in the whole court process and this entailed following attorneys and their cases from one department to another. I spent one day to two weeks observing in sixteen of the trial departments, and I spent two months in one of the short cause departments.[13] This department was known by some as "the plea bargaining court" and cases were frequently transferred there from other courtrooms. While observing in short cause, I thus learned about the other trial departments, as attorneys coming in with their cases would describe their own departments to me and explain why they had transferred to short cause. This period in short cause was at the beginning of my observation and it proved to be very useful because of the contacts I made there with prosecutors and public defenders from the other courtrooms.

One limitation on my field techniques was my having had less contact with private defense attorneys than with public defenders and prosecutors. The private attorneys were usually under a time pressure to move on at the conclusion of their cases, so they did not linger for informal discussions the way the others would. Thus my material on private attorneys is based more upon observation and formal interviews than on informal talks.

A problem for any ethnographer in complex society is: how does one distinguish one cultural scene from all the others in a situation where everyone (superficially, at least) seems to share the same "culture"? Spradley and McCurdy (1972:24) contrast *cultural scenes* with *recurrent social situations,* and suggest that, while the two are closely related, they should not be confused. The cultural scene "is the knowledge which actors employ in a social situation," while the social situation refers to "the observable place, events, objects and persons seen by an investigator" (Spradley and McCurdy 1972:27).

In beginning my fieldwork in the Los Angeles criminal courts, I was not sure what kind of cultural differences there would be. Initially I watched the "recurrent social situation" of attorneys, judges, defendants, clerks, and others coming to court to engage in formal legal proceedings and to interact informally in hallways and during court recesses. After my first month of observation and discussion with various participants, I found that there were at least two distinct "cultural scenes" in court. One pertained to the court regulars—the judges, district attorneys, public defenders, many of the private defense attorneys, and the most experienced of the court staff. They all shared a common definition of the experiences in court and, to an extent, they shared criteria for evaluation and judgment.[14] These regular court participants distinguished themselves from the nonregulars—those participants who appeared less frequently in court, who did not share in the cultural knowledge of the court, and who did not have ongoing social relationships with the regulars. The nonregular participants included some private attorneys, defendants, jurors, police officers, victims, and other witnesses called to testify in cases.[15]

Essentially this dichotomy was between those actors who worked full-time with the court's business and those who did not. The perspective of the regulars was dominated by the attorneys who used legal language to convey social and cultural meanings about cases and court procedures. In the chapters which follow, I describe the social process of settling cases in terms of the language and culture of the regular court participants. As a result, I do not present the defendant's perspective. Defendants ultimately make the decision whether to plead guilty or go to trial, but their decision is heavily influenced by their attorneys. Where a defendant decides in opposition to his attorney's advice, there is said to be a "client-control" problem. The term itself, as it is used by the court regulars, indicates the status of defendants. Although defendants provide the reason for the court's existence, they do not share directly in the culture of the court.

In order to present the perspective of the courtroom culture, I quote extensively from the participants themselves, based upon my field notes. I took notes on (but did not tape-record) most of my observations and all formal interviews. Note-taking was difficult in some situations, however—in hallways, riding the elevators, or while joining attorneys for lunch or drinks after work. I made it a point to jot down brief notes shortly after these conversations and then, each night, I would expand these notes to recreate the discussion as accurately as possible. To protect the identity of my informants, I have used fictitious names and courtroom numbers throughout the book.

Finally, before describing the overall plan of the book, let me note a few of its limits. First, I did not investigate the actions of police or prosecutors in deciding whether to charge a suspect or in determining the nature of the charge. Instead, my research focused on the cases after the formal filing of charges in court. Secondly, the material here describes the culture and process of the court in Los Angeles as it was in 1970-71. I have indicated in the text (or in notes) some changes in the process that have occurred since that time, including: a sharp drop in the number of minor felony offenses and drug cases filed in superior court; a virtual end to the use of submission on the transcript trials; a change in prosecutorial policy on sentence bargaining; and the significant new statute, in 1977, replacing indeterminate sentencing with determinate sentencing.[16] I have not studied the impact of these changes, but simply note them for the reader. Finally, of course, this is a case study of one court system: the courtroom culture and plea bargaining patterns described here pertain only to the felony disposition process in downtown Los Angeles. I do, however, compare my findings with studies of felony courts in other jurisdictions.

The following chapter introduces the main participants in the Los Angeles criminal court process and presents some of the informal knowledge shared by judges, prosecutors, and defense attorneys. Chapter 3 then describes the different kinds of cases according to the categories participants use to organize and define their work. In this chapter I develop a kind of folk taxonomy of cases based upon the seriousness of a case and the strength of the prosecution's case. In chapter 4, I present an overview of the entire court process, showing how the categorization of cases is related to pretrial decisions and patterns of case disposition.

The next two chapters describe numerous cases to show the dynamics of the case disposition process. Defense attorneys shared an understanding of which cases "ought" to be tried and which "ought" to be settled without trial. Chapter 5 (on "light" cases) and chapter 6 (on "serious" cases) describe this defense attorney norm, showing the importance of the strength and seriousness of a case, and the convergence or divergence of defense attorney and prosecutor views on expected outcomes. In chapter 7 I discuss variation among defense attorneys in the advice they gave to their clients, as well as the defendant's role in agreeing to the recommended trial or plea bargain. I chose the cases described in these three chapters according to how well they illustrated the different kinds of dispositions I had observed. In presenting the case materials, I have no doubt that others might comment on, or analyze, the cases differently than I have done. Indeed, I hope and encourage other scholars to do so. A major value of this research is that it gives a close-up look at one courtroom culture, including the everyday routine behaviors as well as the participants' understanding and organization of those behaviors. In chapter 8 I conclude by summarizing the major findings of this research and discussing some of the implications of the work.

2

The Key Participants in Court

This chapter introduces the main participants in the Los Angeles criminal court process. One purpose of the chapter is simply to describe these actors and their organizational structures, and to suggest some of the variables which may affect case disposition. Thus I describe the recruitment, promotion, and organizational constraints on judges, prosecutors, and public defenders. I also discuss characteristics of private defense attorneys and defendants. A second, more important purpose of the chapter is to begin to show how an ethnographic approach leads to a more complete understanding of the court process—one provided by the cultural perspectives of the regular court participants. Thus I present some of the informal knowledge and beliefs shared by attorneys and judges, and suggest how they used this knowledge to shape and interpret their own actions and the actions of others.

Judges

Municipal and superior court judges in California are generally selected by gubernatorial appointment, even though the state formally provides for an elective method of judicial recruitment. The governor appoints judges to fill vacancies as judges retire or die, or to fill new positions authorized by the state legislature. After this initial appointment, judges appear before the voters in nonpartisan elections every six years. Incumbent judges are seldom opposed in these elections, however (Cook 1967:44-45).

In 1970 there were 134 judges for the Superior Court of Los Angeles County. Each year the judges in Los Angeles would elect, by mail ballot, their presiding judge and assistant presiding judge. The actual power of the presiding judge in Los Angeles was quite limited, especially in contrast to the centralized control of other large urban courts, such as Chicago (Balbus 1973:32). In Los Angeles, the presiding judge's only real power lay in the assignment of judges to various courts and in the appointment of the supervising judges for the branch courts and the specialized legal divisions of the central district.

All of the judges annually submitted written requests to the presiding judge stating their preferred court assignment for the year. The presiding judge then tried "to match judicial manpower needs with judicial temperament and preferences," according to an assistant to the executive officer of the court. But this system of assigning judges to their various courtrooms each year also revealed some of the internal politics of the court once one knew how the judges themselves perceived and interpreted their assignments. For example, the civil courts were generally preferred by judges over the criminal courts. And further, within the criminal courts downtown, courts in the Hall of Justice were more desirable than the courts in the Brunswig Building or in the Old Hall of Records. One judge explained how judges were assigned to their respective courts:

> Rank has its privilege. Seniority counts—here and everywhere else. In the superior court, the "low man on the totem pole" goes first to the oldest building to handle criminal matters. Later on you move up to the Hall of Justice. The cases in this building [Hall of Justice] are heavier. . . . After a few years you go over to the new courthouse for the civil matters, unless you choose to stay in criminal. A few do stay here in criminal.

An assistant to the executive officer said that it was not necessarily true that the newer judges began in criminal and then moved up to civil. But then he added:

> It is true that most new judges come from civil practices, so we like to put them in criminal to teach them some criminal law. But there's no policy or rule to that effect.

To an extent, then, judicial assignments reflected the seniority of the judges. Changes in a judge's assignment could also reflect displeasure with the behavior of a particular judge. One court commissioner,[1] assigned to the Brunswig Building, observed that each judge had complete autonomy in his decisions, and then he added:

> If there's something obvious about a judge's conduct, then he might be called in by the presiding judge for a little chat. I don't know. Nothing has ever happened to me. It could of course affect the nature of your court assignment, that is, what courtroom you're in. The newer judges are usually assigned here in the Brunswig Building. So I suppose if you found an old, senior judge sitting over here, then you might suspect something. [This last remark was made with a sardonic laugh.]

There were occasional rumors around the courts about how the district attorney's office or the public defender's office had influenced the presiding judge to transfer certain judges out of the criminal courts. For example, one deputy public defender described a judge he had worked before the previous year:[2]

> He's a very fair man. Really listened to defendants and he didn't just automatically take the [police] officer's word for what happened. He had no compunction about dismissing cases. There were a lot of

acquittals in his court. Of course he ran into trouble, too. . . . Now he's over in Department E. That's for psychiatric and narcotics cases—"nuts and hypes," they call it. He didn't want to go there. He wanted to stay with criminal trials. But out he went.

During 1970 the supervising judge for the criminal courts downtown was responsible for assigning cases to their respective trial departments after the arraignment in Department A, the master calendar department.[3] In making the case assignments, the supervising judge considered administrative factors such as the earliest trial dates being given to defendants in custody, security problems of transferring prisoners out of the Hall of Justice, the availability of public defenders in different trial departments, and the judges' vacation days. The supervising judge exercised some discretion in making case assignments, with particular concern for the assignment of serious cases such as homicide, robbery, heroin, and child molestation. The judge also considered the number of cases each trial department was *actually* handling, in terms of case transfer figures and jury waivers, so that some trial departments would receive a higher number of initial case assignments in recognition of their higher "productivity."

According to attorneys I spoke with, the assignment of different types of cases to their trial departments had important political implications in terms of the judge's status in the judicial hierarchy. One deputy district attorney said:

The way to tell which judges are on their way up—you know, which ones are getting into that clique of judges that runs the system, is to look at which judges get the good cases. Which ones really get the plums? *It's the serious cases—you know, the important ones, the interesting cases—that go to the judges who are on their way up.*

Look at [Judge] King, for example. He got the . . . case [a heavily publicized murder]. And King is over in the Brunswig Building, so you wouldn't think he'd get it. [Judge] Smith got the . . . case [another heavily publicized murder]. . . . *That's the way to tell which judges are in charge—by which cases they get* [emphasis added].

When I commented that only a small percentage of the cases seemed to be significant for their assignment, the deputy district attorney responded:

Yeah, but that's the way it is. Those are the only important cases. You've seen this court [a department in the Brunswig Building] and the cases that come through here. All the crap, the dreck; I mean these cases, most of them are just shit.

A public defender similarly described how his courtroom received only "garbage" cases, in contrast to other courtrooms which had "heavy" cases. Thus, as the attorneys and judges viewed their work, there was a clear difference in the relative importance of various criminal cases. This shared perception of the cases not only affected the decisions on case assignment, but it also provided a cultural meaning for those assignment decisions.

In summary, many of the judges sitting in the criminal courts downtown were biding their time until they could "move up" to a more prestigious court assignment (such as the civil courts or particular branch courts). And within the criminal courts, judges preferred to sit in the Hall of Justice, where more of the interesting and serious cases were assigned. The supervising judge for the criminal courts attempted to assign cases randomly among the various trial departments, with the qualification that he was sensitive to administrative concerns of keeping the cases moving, and to other concerns involving the more serious cases. Thus, judges with less seniority, and/or those with less prestige within an informal judicial hierarchy, tended to receive the less significant cases.

Prosecutors

The district attorney for the County of Los Angeles, selected in nonpartisan elections, has essentially a political and administrative job. The district attorney represents the prosecutorial activities of his office to the public and supervises a large organization of attorneys, investigators, and clerical staff. In 1970 there were 428 attorneys in the office. The district attorney personally appointed only the top two positions in his office. All the other positions were recruited and promoted through civil service.

The deputy district attorneys (hereafter D.A.s) began their work at either grade I or grade II, depending upon their previous experience. Promotions from grade I to grade II were fairly routine, after about a year in the office. Promotion to grades III and IV were made upon the basis of a written examination, evaluation of the deputy's work by his supervisors, and oral interviews. The deputies in grade V positions were in charge of special divisions and branch offices. Attorneys were promoted to the higher grades only as vacancies arose.

Within the central district, responsibility for prosecution was divided into three divisions, corresponding to the main phases of the court proceedings: complaints; preliminary hearings; and felony trials. In the complaints division, D.A.s were usually grade III or IV; their responsibility was to screen arrests brought by police and to decide upon the appropriate charges for prosecution. In the preliminary hearing division, the deputies were generally grade I or II and were supervised by senior deputies. They handled initial arraignments in municipal court and preliminary hearings on all felony cases. Following the preliminary hearing, cases were sent to the group of D.A.s in felony trials for plea bargaining, trials, and sentencing hearings.

There were about seventy deputy D.A.s in felony trials, each assigned to one of the twenty-six courtrooms. The D.A. assignments were rotated annually along with the change in judicial assignments. In each trial department, one grade IV D.A. was appointed to be "calendar deputy" (occasionally this was a grade III), and a grade III and a grade II deputy were assigned there as well. The calendar deputy supervised the work of the junior deputies, kept track of all the cases in his department, and assigned the cases to be handled by each of them. Generally the more serious and complex cases were prosecuted by the more senior deputies.

The exact method of assigning cases to D.A.s and the degree of supervision by the calendar deputy varied with each department. One D.A. described the situation in his department:

> For us, Warren [the calendar deputy] always said, "Anything you see that you like, just take it." We'd sit around when the cases came in and take dibs. But in other departments it's quite formal. Like Garber or that tall guy down the hall. There are some old school ways, you know, where the calendar deputy won't hardly talk to a grade II.

This D.A. added, however, that he thought that most of the departments were informal in the relationships among the deputies. The social distinctions accruing to seniority were more pronounced in the past, he said, and most were gone now.

Since the main concern of this study was prosecution by the seventy deputy D.A.s in felony trials, it is important to note the limitations on their discretion. In other studies, it has been suggested that prosecuting attorneys have a great deal of independence in deciding whether to dismiss cases or reduce charges in exchange for a guilty plea (Enker 1967; Castberg 1968; Alschuler 1968). But in Los Angeles the D.A.s had a set of strict office policies, spelled out in their manuals and periodic directives, to establish some uniformity in plea bargaining.[4] No deputy was allowed to dismiss a case, to take a plea to a misdemeanor, or to take a plea to a reduced felony charge without the approval of one of the two heads of trials (who supervised all of the D.A.s in the felony trials division). Some reductions were approved fairly routinely, while others were more difficult. Much of the learning for new deputies in trials consisted of anticipating what would be considered "appropriate" and thereby "approved" as a nontrial disposition.

Rules on narcotics cases were enforced within the D.A.'s office with particular concern in 1970. Several attorneys told me informally that the D.A.'s policies had tightened up because the district attorney of Los Angeles County was running for the office of Attorney General of California. Defense attorneys said that they were formerly able to plead defendants charged with marijuana possession (Health and Safety Code Sec. 11530) to the lesser, misdemeanor charge of Health and Safety Code Sec. 11556 (being present where marijuana is used). However, this once-routine "deal" was no longer available because of the

election year. A D.A. who had been in the office fourteen years explained why
the policy change had occurred:

> Last year the mayor's committee came out with a report that we had a
> soft line on narcotics. So during the campaign things have tightened up.
> After all, the district attorney is a political animal and he has a lot of
> pressure on him. So he has to make sure that all his deputies will act in
> accordance with the same policies. We used to reduce a possession for
> sale to a simple possession, or strike the priors on a narcotics charge, or
> take a plea to 11556 on a 11530. But the D.A. was getting criticized for
> that.
>
> Personally, I think that a deputy should have the discretion to do these
> things, in certain circumstances. I mean, if the facts warrant it, we
> should be able to compromise. . . . But I can't fault the district attorney
> for these policies, as long as the system is this way, where he's running
> for election and is politically accountable to the public. Drugs are a
> very controversial issue right now.

The difficulties of such administrative attempts to control and order
prosecutorial behavior are discussed in Carter's (1974) study of prosecution in
another California county. The district attorney in that county was rather
unsuccessful in his attempt to establish regular, uniform programming of the
decisions of deputy prosecutors. Carter suggests several factors involving the
technology and environment of prosecutors to explain this failure to develop
ordered procedures for criminal-case disposition. Some of Carter's analysis
applies equally to prosecution in Los Angeles, since, as is discussed below, there
were strategies used by D.A.s to circumvent the formal office policies. Nevertheless, the district attorney in Los Angeles was remarkably successful in ordering
prosecutorial decisions according to the rules and procedures established by
superiors within the office. For example, to enforce internal office control, all
D.A.s in Los Angeles were required to fill out an "alibi sheet" for any case lost
at trial or dismissed, to explain why they think it was lost. Records were also
kept by supervisors in the D.A.'s office on charge reductions and other plea
bargains negotiated by each deputy, in order to insure some accountability. One
D.A. explained:

> The head of trials never gets mad if you lose a case. That could happen
> to anyone. But you'll really get burned if you make a [nontrial]
> disposition when you shouldn't have. In other words, when you go
> beyond your authority, you'll get reprimanded, but not when you
> make an error.

Although these rules and regulations within the D.A.'s office did present
real constraints on the deputies' behavior, there were in fact ways to circumvent

some of the official policies. The prosecutors were supposed to obtain written approval from one of the heads of trials for any charge reduction or dismissal. However, for certain charges which appeared frequently, the reductions were approved so routinely that deputy D.A.s might seek written approval *after* the fact of the reduction. One calendar deputy D.A. noted that he didn't need approval because

> sometimes I sit in for the chief of trials upstairs and then I'm making all these decisions myself, so there's no point for me to ask ahead of time. But I'm not really a fair example. Now Dick here [nodding to his junior colleague D.A.], he's been taking pleas and *then* sending them up the next day for approval on them, where clearly he shouldn't be. [This was said in a teasing way, not in a reprimand.]

Although the paperwork for official approval of charge reduction was sometimes manipulated in this way, the fact of formal supervision remained. For example, a grade II D.A. described an encounter with one of the heads of trials:

> On a case last year, he called me in to ask why I had made a particular disposition on a pill case. There was conflicting evidence on the case. The police arrest report said there were sixteen pills, but at the preliminary hearing the officer said there were only twelve pills. So I wrote "twelve pills" in my report on the disposition. The head of trials said, "Put down ten pills." You see, this was because office policy is that you can only dispose of a case [to a misdemeanor charge] where there are ten pills or less.

If an individual D.A. considered that a particular plea bargain, or nontrial disposition, was appropriate in a case and yet he was not sure that his superiors would approve it, he had several options. One possibility was to go to his superiors and argue vigorously for approval of the suggested disposition. For example, one D.A. said that he was rarely denied permission to dispose of a case the way he wanted. Then he added:

> It's true Parsons [one of the heads of trials] is very hard-nosed. But then I just don't take "no" for an answer, so I've never been turned down. I'm a fighter, that's all.

Some D.A.s were on better terms with their superiors than others; thus there was also an element of variability in approval according to the personal relationships among the prosecutors.

To avoid dealing with their D.A. superiors, individual prosecutors could enlist the aid of the judge to arrange a nontrial disposition. One way of doing this was for the calendar deputy D.A. to amend the information to add an agreed-upon lesser charge against the defendant. The defendant and his attorney would then submit the case to the judge for adjudication based upon the transcript of the preliminary hearing. This procedure, called "submission on the transcript" (S.O.T.), frequently substituted for a plea of guilty. Typically the judge would acquit the defendant of the original charge but convict him on this new, lesser charge. A public defender described how this procedure worked in his trial department:

> Well, off the record, we've got a good thing going in this department, because the D.A.s don't check into their head office. What we do is go into chambers and get the judge to do it [that is, reduce or dismiss charges]. Like if we have a sale case and we want possession, if the D.A. here were to phone over to his office, they'd probably deny it and then it would be very difficult to talk to the judge after that. . . . So our D.A.s don't even phone over there. We'll go over to the judge and talk to him. Then S.O.T. it and the judge will come back guilty on the lesser charge.

The public defender added that there could be no objection from the D.A. head office, "because it's the judge who did it."

The S.O.T. proceeding was also used by prosecutors in order to dismiss charges without going through their superiors. One D.A. told me he wished he could dismiss a case he was prosecuting,

> but I can't because of the bureaucracy. They [the head office] say, "If *we* choose to file on this case, then *you* had better see it through." So all I can do is put it on. There should be some way to get rid of it, but I'm the newest here—even below the regular junior man—so I can't do it. Jack, our calendar deputy, probably could. But even him, they give so much crap over there on any dismissal.

Many D.A.s who wanted to dismiss a case would use the S.O.T. proceeding as a "slow" plea of *not* guilty, instead of seeking permission to dismiss the case. That is, a D.A. would explain his feelings to the judge on why the case should be thrown out and then the judge would acquit the defendant in an S.O.T. trial. This way the individual D.A. would have less responsibility for the outcome.[5]

Interestingly, the D.A.'s office later discovered this widespread use of the S.O.T. procedure to avoid internal constraints on plea bargaining. The study of Greenwood and associates (1973) received considerable publicity in the Los Angeles newspapers showing, among other things, the lenient dispositions received by the defendants convicted in S.O.T. trials. The D.A.'s office began to monitor closely the use of S.O.T. by deputy prosecutors and, at the beginning of 1974, issued a formal memorandum which virtually prohibited S.O.T. dispositions. As testimony to the effectiveness of such internal constraints, one finds a sharp decrease in the percentage of cases in Los Angeles disposed of by S.O.T. In 1970, trial by submission on the transcript accounted for 32.3 percent of the dispositions in superior court, but in 1974 only 2.5 percent of the dispositions were by S.O.T. trials.[6]

In summary, it is important to recognize that the prosecutors in Los Angeles did not have total discretion to dispose of cases as they saw fit. Instead, they were limited by the official policies of the D.A. office and, to an extent, they were limited by their position within the hierarchy of the D.A. organization. However, there were ways that a D.A. could overcome these constraints, either by persistence within the office or by the aid of the trial judge.

Defense Attorneys

As in most urban criminal courts, a great many of the defendants in Los Angeles were indigent and unable to afford the cost of a private attorney. Within the central district, the public defender's office represented about 70 percent of defendants in 1970. Roughly 5 to 8 percent of defendants downtown were represented by court-appointed attorneys—private attorneys appointed by the court to represent indigent defendants who, for one reason or other, could not be represented by the public defender. The remainder of defendants were represented by privately retained counsel (except for an occasional defendant who represented himself, *propria persona*).

Public Defenders

The Los Angeles County Public Defender's Office, established in 1913, is the oldest public defender office in the country. It is also the largest office in the country; in 1970 about 500 persons were employed there, including 355 attorneys, 45 investigators, and about 100 clerical and other nonlegal staff. The public defender himself is appointed by the Los Angeles County Board of Supervisors, and all employees are recruited and promoted through civil service with the county. The deputy public defenders (hereafter P.D.s) have the same set of grades (I, II, III, IV, and head deputies) with the same salary scale as deputies in the D.A.'s office. The P.D.s are promoted on the basis of written examination, personnel evaluations and years of experience, as vacancies occur in the higher grades of the office. The P.D.'s office and the D.A.'s office both tended to recruit high-quality recent law-school graduates (there was some disagreement as to which office attracted higher-quality recruits), offering a starting salary (in 1970) of about $12,000 to a graduate with no experience. Both offices also had a fairly high turnover of deputies.[7]

The public defender's office divided responsibility for defense of cases in the central district in a manner similar to the division for prosecutors. There was one group of P.D.s assigned to handle preliminary hearings in municipal court;

these P.D.s were usually grade I or II and they worked under the supervision of a senior P.D. A second, more experienced group of P.D.s handled the defense in superior court; these P.D.s, in the felony trials division, were typically grade III or IV deputies. There were about fifty deputy P.D.s in felony trials, with roughly two P.D.s in each trial department.

The chief of trials supervised all P.D.s in felony trials and assigned cases to each on the basis of the deputy's workload and experience. P.D.s generally handled four cases per week—one scheduled for each day with a fifth day free for interviewing clients and witnesses. The more serious cases were assigned to the more experienced P.D.s within each department. As the chief of trials went through this process of case assignment one afternoon (with about forty cases), he explained to me how the "light" cases could be assigned "to anyone," while "the heavy cases go to a grade IV deputy."

The determination of how "heavy" a case was seemed to depend first upon the offense type. For example, the chief of trials picked up two case transcripts assigned to one department, one involving burglary and the other pills, and noted that "a burglary is heavier than a pill case"; he then assigned the pill case to the P.D. with the least seniority in that department. In another set, the chief of trials noted that "a robbery is heavier than a burglary," and he continued in this way, matching cases with P.D.s. In making the assignments, the chief of trials also considered any allegation of prior felony convictions. "Priors" had to be alleged by the D.A. at the time of the arraignment and, if found true at trial, they would increase the eventual sentence on a defendant. A burglary with two priors alleged was "heavier" than a burglary with no priors and was assigned accordingly to the more senior deputy. Finally, the chief of trials gave special attention to cases which involved a possible death penalty. "These cases," he said, "are the really heavy ones. They're either homicide or [P.C. Sec.] 209—kidnapping with bodily injury." Possible death-penalty cases were assigned to grade IV deputies, even if it required shifting a P.D. from his regular trial department.

This practice of assigning the "heavier" or more serious cases to the more experienced attorneys was followed in both the P.D. and D.A. offices. Note that the pattern was similar to that for judicial case assignments, where the more serious cases tended to be assigned to judges with more seniority.

The P.D.s in felony trials did not have organizational policies with respect to their defense of a case similar to the constraints on the D.A.s. The P.D.s were quick to point this out, to contrast their office with the D.A.'s office. As one P.D. said, "We owe allegiance to no one except our client." Another noted, "We do whatever *we* think is appropriate in defending a client." There were, however, frequent discussions among the P.D.s where they informally shared advice on case strategies. One P.D. did mention two points which, he said, could possibly be considered policies for the office.

First we have to make motions—argue any pretrial issues—wherever appropriate. Even if they're weak and might be denied. And the second thing is, in heroin cases which involve police informants, P.D.s must insist on securing the informant. . . .

The P.D.s frequently argued pretrial motions, such as on constitutional issues of search and seizure, partly in order to protect the record for any appeal.

Private Defense Attorneys

The private defense bar in Los Angeles can be divided into the lawyer "regulars" and the "nonregulars," where the "regulars" handle a high volume of criminal cases and are seen frequently in criminal court. Because of the geographic decentralization of Los Angeles, there are actually several groups of "regulars" surrounding each of the branch courts as well as a group of lawyers who generally practice around the criminal court downtown. The existence of lawyer "regulars" has been noted in studies of other urban criminal courts, as "regular" criminal attorneys handle the bulk of the nonindigent caseload and frequently maintain close ties with bail bondsmen and court officials (Blumberg 1967; Wood 1956; and Carlin 1962).

In Los Angeles, as elsewhere, informal relationships and mutual trust were important to working out case dispositions and so, as one D.A. put it:

The best thing for a defense attorney is that he mix well with the criminal law community. He shouldn't be a lone wolf or a shyster. He should be able to walk into the D.A.'s office or the city attorney's office and he'd have some friends there. He should be able to walk into courtrooms and the clerks would know him by first name. He's got to be willing to become a part of the community he's working in. Then he can do a lot for his client.

A comment which I heard several times was, "The best private attorneys are the ex-D.A.s and ex-P.D.s." Naturally, those were the attorneys who had been part of that crucial "criminal law community," as well as having had extensive experience with criminal law. The "nonregular" attorneys appeared only occasionally in criminal court and generally lacked experience with the informal practices of the court. These attorneys often handled primarily civil cases or else they were just starting their law practice and were handling whatever cases they could.

Private defense attorneys generally handled criminal cases on the basis of a fixed fee per case; that is, the client paid the same fee for his attorney's services whether the case was settled by a guilty plea or a full trial. While this was the norm, some attorneys did set two fees, with a higher one for a trial disposition. The typical fixed-fee method of compensation provided a strong incentive for private attorneys to settle their cases in the least time-consuming way so that they could have a higher turnover of cases. As one private attorney (a courtroom "regular") commented, "It's a volume business." The actual fees varied among defense attorneys and their clientele, with one attorney noting, "We charge what the traffic will bear."

Private defense attorneys were also appointed by the court to represent indigent defendants who could not be represented by the P.D. Usually this occurred in multi-defendant cases, where there was a conflict of interest if the P.D. were to represent both defendants in the case. These court appointments were authorized by P.C. Sec. 987a, and the attorneys were paid by the court on an hourly basis for their services. One P.D. characterized Sec. 987a attorneys as follows:

> 987a attorneys run the gamut completely from new guys just starting out in practice to ex-P.D.s or D.A.s with a great deal of expertise who are just starting to build a criminal practice of their own. Court appointments don't pay as well as fees for most private attorneys with big practices. So it's often for the guys just starting out. The balance are known to the judge and he chooses them. . . . You don't see the most common criminal lawyers seeking 987a appointments. . . . They have a big criminal practice already. So they wouldn't need 987a work—unless they're right there in court and do it as a favor to the judge.

Comparison of Defense Attorney Caseloads

Skolnick (1967:64-67) emphasized differences in the characteristics of defendants represented by the public defender and by private defense attorneys, suggesting that critics of the public defender have often failed to consider these differences when comparing the case dispositions for the different types of attorneys. Indeed, in Los Angeles, the public defender represented proportionately more defendants with substantial prior criminal records and more defendants under existing criminal status (such as probation or parole) than did private attorneys (Smith 1970:49-54).[8] Smith's (1970:49-51) study of all felony dispositions in Los Angeles in 1968 also showed that 55 percent of the P.D. clients remained in jail pending their case disposition, compared to only 17.4 percent of clients of private attorneys. Thus, to the extent that being in custody limits a defendant's ability to aid in his own defense, this limitation was felt more severely by clients of the P.D. than by private attorney clients.

In terms of the offense charged, the P.D. handled proportionately more robbery, burglary, and forgery and checks cases, while private attorneys had proportionately more murder, rape, other sex offenses, and marijuana cases.

Also, the P.D. represented proportionately more black and Mexican-American defendants than did the private attorneys (Smith 1970:44-50).

Defendants

Defendants generally did not share in the informal knowledge and work routines of the court. Thus, this section presents basic demographic data on felony defendants in Los Angeles County, drawing especially on reports from the California Bureau of Criminal Statistics (hereafter B.C.S.).[9]

Most felony defendants in Los Angeles were relatively young, with 51.2 percent in 1970 under age twenty-five, and only 11.2 percent forty and over (B.C.S. 1970a).[10] The vast majority of defendants were male; in 1969 only 12.2 percent of defendants were female (B.C.S. 1969). Further, 52.3 percent of defendants in 1970 were Anglo-American, 12.6 percent Mexican-American, 34.0 percent black, and 1.1 percent other (B.C.S. 1970a). The proportion of minority-group defendants was much higher in the central district than for the entire county. For example, Greenwood and associates (1976:58) reported the ethnic distribution of defendants in each court district for a sample of 2,617 burglary and robbery defendants in 1970, showing that only 35.1 percent of the defendants in the central district were Anglo-American, while 53.2 percent were black and 11.7 percent were Mexican-American.

A significant proportion of felony defendants in Los Angeles in 1970 had some type of prior criminal record: 14.3 percent had a prison record; 29.6 percent had a "major" record (convictions with sentences of at least ninety days in jail, or probation for over one year but with no time in prison); 33.8 percent had a "minor" record (ranging from one known arrest to convictions with sentences of less than ninety days in jail or up to one year probation); and 22.3 percent had no record (no known arrest or conviction) (B.C.S. 1970a). In addition, some defendants were already under formal supervision (that is, had an existing criminal status) at the time they were prosecuted in 1970. Of the total number of defendants for whom existing criminal status was reported, 30.8 percent were under some type of commitment, either probation, parole, or institutional commitment (B.C.S. 1970a).

Defendants were most commonly charged with drug offenses. In 1970, a very high proportion—43.8 percent—of all felony defendants in Los Angeles were prosecuted for drug law violations, primarily possession of marijuana or dangerous drugs (pills). Since 1970, many of these minor drug cases have been prosecuted as misdemeanors instead of felonies, or else they have been diverted out of the criminal court system. But, in 1970, drug law violations constituted a major group of the felonies in Los Angeles. The next most frequent offense charged was burglary (14.9 percent of all felony defendants in 1970), followed by grand theft—personal and auto (11.6 percent), forgery and checks (6.7

percent), robbery (5.9 percent), assault (5.2 percent), and various other felony offenses (12.0 percent).[11]

The distribution of offenses among the court districts was not entirely uniform. In particular, the central district handled proportionately more of the homicide, opiates, bookmaking, arson, and escape cases, and proportionately fewer of the marijuana and dangerous drug cases. Controversial and newsworthy cases (such as political cases and sensational murders) were generally handled downtown even if they originated elsewhere in the county. These cases were transferred to the central district so as to avoid tying up a branch court in what might be a prolonged trial. Also, major criminal cases that arose from grand jury indictments were heard in the central district.

There was a relationship between the type of offense and some of the defendant characteristics described above. For example, over 60 percent of marijuana, auto theft, and robbery charges involved defendants who were under twenty-five.[12] Bookmaking, on the other hand, was charged against virtually no one under twenty-five, but over 60 percent of bookmaking defendants were forty or over. Drunk driving, other sex offenses (lewd acts with child, sex perversion, and so on) and hit and run involved the next largest proportions of defendants who were forty or over.

Offenses involving the highest proportions of defendants with major criminal records or prison records included escape, robbery, opiates, burglary, auto theft, kidnapping, and deadly weapons. These same offenses generally showed the highest proportions of defendants with existing criminal status (for example, on probation or parole) as well. On the other hand, the offenses of vehicular manslaughter, other sex offenses, marijuana, and hit and run were characterized by high proportions of defendants with no prior criminal record.

Comparing offenses by age and prior record one finds, for example, that marijuana defendants were generally young with no record or only a minor record. Robbery and auto theft defendants were also generally young, but frequently with major or prison records. On the other hand, other sex offenses, hit and run, and vehicular manslaughter tended to involve older defendants with little or no prior record. Although none of these results is surprising in any way, they are important in shaping the identity of felony defendants. Attorneys and judges shared a knowledge of the typical characteristics of defendants charged with different criminal offenses. This social identity of defendants, as perceived and interpreted by the courtroom regulars, played a significant role in the case disposition process, as discussed in the following chapters.

3 Kinds of Cases: Seriousness and Strength

In the previous chapter, I showed how the assignment of a case to individual participants (judges, D.A.s, and P.D.s) was made on the basis of how "serious" or "heavy" the case was. This particular concept—the seriousness of a case—is an integral part of the courtroom culture. The fact that attorneys categorize their cases in this way is crucial not only for explaining organizational assignments, but for explaining pretrial strategies and the choice of disposition method as well. In this chapter I develop a framework for categorization of cases based upon the *seriousness* of a case, and on the additional feature of the *strength* of the prosecution's case. At this point I am simply identifying and describing the general categories. The following chapters will show how these categories are used by attorneys in the actual process of case disposition.

I derived this framework by observing and listening to attorneys talk to each other about their cases. The terms to be presented here are those used by the attorneys themselves as they described their cases and pointed to features justifying or explaining decisions on disposition. In this sense, the terms can be considered part of a *folk taxonomy,* that is, a cognitive ordering and classification of objects into named categories.[1] No formal techniques of componential analysis (for example, questioning by eliciting or asking informants to sort terms) were used to refine and verify the categories. Thus the framework presented here is not a true folk taxonomy in the strict sense. Instead it is advanced as an analytical typology based upon my observation of the language and behavior of the attorneys.

Seriousness

The seriousness of a case refers to a prediction by attorneys of the severity of the sentence to be imposed upon conviction. A "serious" case is one with a high chance of state prison sentence. A "light" case is one with no real likelihood of state prison and a good chance of a sentence of probation. In order to understand the full meaning of these categories, one must know more about the sentencing decision—what the alternative sentences are, the degree of variation among judges in sentencing, and the determinants of the sentence. Such information is presented below. Normally discussion of sentencing is presented after a discussion of disposition rather than before. However, to provide an ethnographic explanation of the disposition process, I must describe the process as the participants themselves understand it, that is, a process in large measure shaped by the anticipation of punishment. Attorneys make predictions on probable sentences; they categorize their cases based upon these predictions; and *then* they decide upon pretrial strategies and methods of disposition.

In the following discussion of sentencing, I first describe the relevant California statutes and correctional institutions. The next two sections discuss the sentencing process in Los Angeles and the factors determining the sentence. Finally, I summarize how attorneys use this information to make predictions on expected severity of punishment, that is, how attorneys categorize cases according to seriousness.

The California Sentencing System

In 1970-71, California had a system of indeterminate sentencing, by which the actual length of a defendant's prison sentence was determined by an administrative body, the Adult Authority, not by the sentencing judge.[2] Thus a convicted offender was sent to prison (the Department of Corrections) simply "for the term prescribed by law" (P.C. Sec. 1168). The penal code prescribed a minimum and maximum term for each offense, but these terms gave the Adult Authority broad discretion in setting an offender's actual release date (for example, a second-degree robbery term was one year to life; an assault with a deadly weapon term was one to fifteen years).

The Department of Corrections operated thirteen major institutions (ranging from minimum- to maximum-security facilities) and over thirty forestry camps (Wright 1973:58). When offenders entered prison, they were classified according to their potential for rehabilitation and their need for security. Then they were assigned to one of the correctional institutions in the state. This classification system and the indeterminate sentence allowed the prison administrators and the Adult Authority a great deal of control over inmates. The Adult Authority fixed a prisoner's release date according to when he had been "rehabilitated" (Wright 1973:44). This same administrative body had the power to grant parole, to establish conditions for parole, to revoke parole, and to redetermine the length of the prison sentence if parole were violated (Hitchcock 1972:362). Because of the indeterminate nature of a commitment to the Department of Corrections and the harsh conditions in many of the prisons, defendants and their attorneys perceived a prison sentence to be a very severe commitment.

Judges were not required to send convicted offenders to prison, however. Instead there were a variety of alternative sentences available to the court. When a defendant was convicted of a *mandatory* felony—that is, an offense for which commitment to state prison was prescribed by law—the judge could (with certain restrictions to be noted below): (1) sentence the defendant to state prison,

(2) place him on probation, (3) sentence him to the Department of Mental Hygiene, (4) sentence him to the California Rehabilitation Center, or (5) sentence him to the California Youth Authority.

In order to grant probation to a defendant convicted of a mandatory felony, the judge usually "suspended the proceedings," which meant that imposition of the sentence was postponed. A defendant who violated the conditions of probation then could still be sent to prison at a new sentencing hearing, although usually a defendant would be given another chance on probation. In awarding probation, the court sometimes required the defendant to spend some time (up to one year) in county jail as a condition of probation. Even with jail time, probation was an attractive alternative to prison; but not all defendants were eligible for probation. For example, probation could not be granted to defendants armed with a deadly weapon at the time of a robbery, burglary, or arson, or to defendants with a prior felony conviction, "except in unusual cases where the interests of justice demand a departure" (P.C. Sec. 1203). In other cases (for example, involving a defendant with *two* prior felony convictions), probation could not be granted "except in unusual cases . . . and where the district attorney concurs" (P.C. Sec. 1203).

A defendant convicted of certain sex offenses could be sent to the Department of Mental Hygiene as a "mentally disordered sex offender." This civil commitment was indeterminate in length and could involve confinement for life. Thus mental hygiene, like prison, was perceived as a very severe sentence. Narcotics addicts (or offenders in danger of becoming addicts) could be sentenced to the California Rehabilitation Center (C.R.C.) by civil commitment proceedings. Defendants usually preferred C.R.C. to prison because the term of confinement was generally shorter at C.R.C. and the conditions were better there. Also, there was treatment specifically for addicts. However, C.R.C. was quite selective in which offenders they would accept for their program. For example, defendants with prior records were usually not eligible for C.R.C. commitment. Finally, defendants under twenty-one could be sentenced to the California Youth Authority, a network of correctional institutions and forestry camps for juveniles.

When a defendant was convicted of an *optional* felony—that is, an offense punishable by state prison *or* fine *or* county jail—then the judge had sentencing options *in addition* to these above. The judge could simply fine the defendant or he could sentence the defendant to a straight term of up to one year of county jail (instead of making jail a condition of probation). Examples of *mandatory* felonies were homicide, robbery, first-degree burlgary, and sale of marijuana; examples of *optional* felonies were second-degree burglary, possession of marijuana, grand theft, forgery, and bookmaking.

The chief advantage to defendants of conviction on an optional felony (in addition to the possibility of a more lenient commitment) is that it may result in a misdemeanor—rather than a felony—level of conviction. The level of conviction in California is defined by the type of sentence imposed, not by the charge. According to P.C. Sec. 17(b), an optional felony offense becomes "a misdemeanor for all purposes under the following circumstances": when the court imposes any sentence other than imprisonment in the state prison; when the court sentences a defendant to the youth authority; or when the court grants probation and declares the offense to be a misdemeanor.

A misdemeanor level of conviction is preferable over a felony level of conviction for several reasons. Many extralegal sanctions apply to convicted felons. For example, occupational licensing boards will often refuse licenses to felons but not to misdemeanants. Likewise, the armed services will not accept convicted felons. In addition to these social sanctions, there are strong legal sanctions accompanying a felony conviction. Most importantly, a felony level of conviction counts as a "prior" on any subsequent criminal offense. As noted earlier, defendants with a prior felony conviction are generally not eligible for probation. Also, certain offenses are punishable by higher penalties for defendants with a prior felony conviction.

Sentencing in Los Angeles

Although all of the cases in court, by their definition as felonies, are punishable by state prison, few defendants were in fact sent to prison. Of the 25,642 defendants initially charged with felonies who were convicted in Los Angeles in 1970, only 6 percent were sent to the Department of Corrections; 70 percent were placed on probation (some with jail time), 14.8 percent were sentenced to county jail, and 9.2 percent received other sentences such as youth authority, fine, California Rehabilitation Center, or Department of Mental Hygiene (B.C.S. 1970a).

Further, most defendants initially charged with felonies were convicted at the misdemeanor level in Los Angeles. Recall that the level of conviction is determined by the type of sentence imposed, not by the charge. Of the 25,642 felony defendants convicted in 1970, 59.3 percent received misdemeanor sentences (that is, were convicted at the misdemeanor level) and 40.7 percent received felony sentences. But while 59.3 percent were convicted at the misdemeanor *level*, only 9.1 percent were actually convicted of misdemeanor *charges* (B.C.S. 1970a). The D.A.s were reluctant to reduce charges to misdemeanors in exchange for guilty pleas. They preferred instead to let the judges use their discretion in sentencing to set the conviction at the misdemeanor level. Charge reduction was most important in cases involving mandatory felonies; a guilty plea to a lesser, optional felony would give the court the choice between a misdemeanor or a felony sentence.

To aid the judge in sentencing, a probation report was prepared summarizing the defendant's background and offense. The report included material on the defendant's prior criminal record, education, employment, and family background, and on the circumstances of the offense. The report also included personal letters by the defendant or by anyone interested in his case, and an evaluation of the defendant and recommendation by the probation officer on the suitability of probation.

Defense attorneys occasionally talked to probation officers in order to offer additional information to support a lenient recommendation, but this practice varied with different attorneys. Some attorneys never contacted the probation office; others did so only when they felt it was particularly important; and other attorneys regularly spoke to the officers about their clients. There seemed to be no difference between P.D.s and private attorneys in terms of their contact with the probation officers. Also, the prosecutors had little contact with the probation department and rarely talked to officers doing presentence investigation. If a D.A. had a strong opinion about a defendant's sentence, he would express it directly to the judge, not to the probation officer doing the report.

In some cases all parties agreed to waive the probation report and have the defendant sentenced immediately after conviction. Defendants in custody who anticipated a sentence of probation were particularly interested in immediate sentencing in order to avoid the additional three weeks of custody waiting for completion of the probation report. Agreement on waiver of the probation report was sometimes part of a plea-bargained disposition. In 17.9 percent of the cases in Los Angeles in 1970, the recommendation of the probation officer was "unknown or no recommendation" (B.C.S. 1970c). Presumably most of these cases involved a waiver of the probation report.

Most judges tended to follow sentence recommendations given in the probation report and, to the extent that they did not, it was usually the judges who were more lenient than the probation officers. Judges followed the recommendations of the probation officer, granting or denying probation to 80.7 percent of defendants for whom recommendations were made in 1970 (B.C.S. 1970c). More specifically, where probation *was* recommended, judges followed the recommendations for 96.1 percent of defendants, but where probation was *not* recommended, judges followed the recommendations for only 59.5 percent of defendants, thus awarding probation to a substantial number of defendants for whom probation officers had recommended denial of probation (B.C.S. 1970c). The more lenient sentencing views of judges were usually the result of plea bargaining at the time of case disposition. Particularly if the defendant had been convicted without a full trial, the judge may have already indicated to defense (either formally or informally) what the likely sentence would be. If the probation report recommended a more severe sentence than the judge had previously indicated, he might still choose to proceed with his earlier indication.

The judicial practice of discussing sentencing possibilities with attorneys prior to case disposition is known in Los Angeles as "chamberizing." That is, the

D.A. and defense attorney would go into the judge's chambers to discuss possibilities for nontrial disposition and to obtain an indication from the judge as to what the likely sentence would be. A few judges refused to chamberize. But most agreed to discuss sentencing, differing only on the extent to which they would commit themselves to a specific sentence before the final case disposition.

Some judges gave an indication of their thoughts about sentencing in a particular case, but would not make any commitment or promise to that effect. Other judges would make an actual sentence promise that was conditioned upon a favorable probation report. In the latter instance, the promise, or plea bargain over sentence, was made part of the formal court record at the time of disposition; in the event of an unfavorable probation report which the judge chose to follow, the defendant was allowed to withdraw his guilty plea. The fact that these sentence promises were entered into the court record reflected the recent California Supreme Court decision of *People* v. *West* (91 Cal. Rptr. 385, 1970).

Finally, some judges gave either a prediction of their sentence or a sentence promise according to the facts and circumstances of the individual case. One judge of this type described his feelings about chamberizing as follows:

> *I make very few actual bargains.* But I do go to great lengths to let the attorneys know how I am *thinking* about the case so that they can make some predictions about my decisions. *I will give a good indication as to what sentence this defendant would probably receive,* based upon the facts of the case in the transcript and the attorney's representation of the background and record of the defendant. *But I'm not making any promises.* My final decision on the sentence is not made until after I read the probation report. And this is all explained to the defendant— he is not allowed to withdraw his plea if the sentence turns out to be other than what he expected.
>
> *In some cases I may make a promise* of "no state prison," *but then it will be a clear promise and a bargain* [emphasis added].

This involvement of judges in plea bargaining by way of chamberizing over the sentence is noteworthy because of the emphasis in the criminal justice literature on prosecutorial control over sentencing. For example, studies by Blumberg (1967), Neubauer (1974), and Casper (1972) stress the importance of the prosecutor's sentence recommendation and note the minimal role of the judge in this area.[3] But in Los Angeles the role of the judge was significant, and, in many cases, the prosecutor had no direct concern with sentencing. This judicial dominance was particularly true in "light" cases where judges possessed ample discretion to impose a lenient sentence, and where the defendant's charged offense and lack of prior record indicated the likelihood that probation would be granted. In "serious" cases, the D.A.s played a greater role since, to the extent that they controlled the charge and alleged prior convictions, they determined the sentencing alternatives available to the judge. The D.A.s were also much more likely to make sentence recommendations in "serious" cases.[4] One judge commented:

> In Los Angeles, the D.A. does not generally make any recommendation on sentencing. This is a very unusual practice—it is unlike the rest of the country where the D.A. takes an active role in sentencing. *But here, the defense attorney and the judge bargain*—at least to the extent that bargaining or discussion occurs. . . . Judges take an active role in sentencing. Because of this, any plea bargaining in Los Angeles is different from most other places. Although it is true that *what charge a plea is taken to is controlled by the D.A., not by the judge. So the D.A. enters discussions that way—he controls that decision* [emphasis added].

Factors Determining the Sentence

In order to characterize cases according to expected severity of the sentence, defense and prosecuting attorneys must know how particular cases fit into the general pattern of sentencing decisions. Attorneys, judges, and probation officers all commented that the defendant's prior criminal record and the offense were two key factors determining the sentence.[5]

Defendants without criminal records could anticipate leniency from the court. As one's prior record grew worse, the likelihood of a severe sentence increased. Table 3-1 shows the relationship between prior criminal record and type of commitment for all defendants convicted and sentenced in Los Angeles County in 1970. Sentences involving *no* incarceration (probation without jail or fine) were imposed upon 76.1 percent of defendants with no record and 63.0 percent of defendants with minor records; but these lenient sentences were given to only 38.2 percent of defendants with prior prison records. Likewise, the most severe sentences of state prison or Department of Mental Hygiene were given to 17.3 percent of defendants with prior prison records, 7.2 percent of defendants with major records, 3.0 percent of defendants with minor records, and 1.4 percent of defendants with no record.

A second crucial factor determining the severity of the sentence was the offense. Table 3-2 shows the distribution of sentences by charged offense for defendants convicted and sentenced in Los Angeles County in 1970. Defendants charged with bookmaking, marijuana, other sex offenses, hit and run, other drug offenses, deadly weapons, and dangerous drugs were most likely to receive lenient sentences; over 60 percent of defendants charged with each of those offenses received sentences involving no incarceration—probation without jail or a fine. On the other hand, defendants charged with homicide, kidnapping,

Table 3-1
Type of Commitment, by Defendant's Prior Record, for Defendants Convicted and Sentenced in Superior Court of Los Angeles County, 1970
(percent)

Defendant's Prior Criminal Record	Total Defendants	Type of Commitment							
		Dept. of Corrections	CYA	Probation without Jail	Probation with Jail	Jail	Fine	CRC	Mental Hygiene
No record	100% (N=5,370)	1.1	.8	70.3	14.1	7.3	5.8	.2	.3
Minor record	100% (N=8,649)	3.0	3.5	59.4	22.8	6.9	3.6	1.1	.03
Major record	100% (N=7,771)	7.2	5.5	36.4	24.8	19.6	1.8	4.4	.03
Prison record	100% (N=3,852)	16.9	1.3	23.6	17.8	33.2	.9	5.8	.4
Total	100% (N=25,642)	6.0	3.2	49.3	20.6	14.8	3.1	2.6	.3

Source: Bureau of Criminal Statistics (personal communication, 1971).

Table 3-2
Type of Commitment, by Offense Charged, for Defendants Convicted and Sentenced in Superior Court of Los Angeles County, 1970
(percent)

Offense Charged	Total Defendants	Dept. of Corrections	CYA	Probation without Jail	Probation with Jail	Jail	Fine	CRC	Mental Hygiene
Homicide	316	56.3	4.1	16.8	20.9	1.6	0.0	0.3	0.0
Manslaughter, vehicle	64	7.8	1.6	42.2	42.2	4.7	1.6	0.0	0.0
Robbery	1,582	24.5	13.0	18.5	28.0	12.4	0.4	3.4	0.0
Assault	1,283	6.6	2.9	50.7	22.3	14.2	2.9	0.2	0.2
Burglary	4,104	6.0	4.4	39.1	23.6	21.6	1.1	4.0	0.1
Theft, except auto	1,571	3.2	2.2	50.2	20.8	21.8	1.0	0.7	0.0
Theft, auto	1,302	3.1	4.5	43.3	21.4	26.2	0.7	0.8	0.0
Forgery and checks	1,889	5.3	1.0	55.2	20.2	14.5	0.9	3.0	0.0
Rape, forcible	286	15.7	6.6	33.2	25.5	14.0	0.0	0.0	4.9
Other sex offenses	605	5.6	0.5	54.9	9.3	11.9	8.3	0.2	9.4
Total drug violations	10,858	2.4	2.1	58.2	19.7	10.7	3.6	3.3	0.0
Opiates	972	13.8	1.7	29.3	19.0	5.6	0.4	30.1	0.0
Marijuana	4,039	0.8	1.5	66.5	17.7	8.3	5.1	0.2	0.0
Dangerous drugs	5,671	1.7	2.7	57.2	21.3	13.1	3.2	0.8	0.0
Other drug violations	176	1.7	1.1	59.1	15.3	17.0	2.8	2.8	0.0
Deadly weapons	287	2.8	0.3	52.3	10.1	25.8	8.7	0.0	0.0
Drunk driving	353	1.7	0.0	46.5	28.3	15.6	4.0	4.0	0.0
Hit and run	100	1.0	2.0	60.0	23.0	11.0	3.0	0.0	0.0
Escape	138	1.4	0.7	9.4	4.3	81.9	1.4	0.7	0.0
Kidnapping	156	39.7	3.8	21.8	25.0	9.0	0.0	0.6	0.0
Bookmaking	560	0.0	0.0	65.0	1.3	1.8	32.0	0.0	0.0
Other	188	10.1	4.3	51.6	25.0	6.9	2.1	0.0	0.0
Total	25,642	6.0	3.2	49.3	20.6	14.8	3.1	2.6	0.3

Source: Administrative Offices of Superior Court of Los Angeles.

robbery, and forcible rape were most likely to receive severe commitments of state prison or mental hygiene.

Of course, one would expect sentencing to vary by offense type, since the penal code prescribes different penalties for different offenses. However, besides statutory differences, the actual variation in sentencing reflected the judges' views on the severity of different crimes. Cases were perceived according to categories of "normal crime"—categories of offense types based upon knowledge of typical patterns in committing such offenses and the characteristics of the typical offender associated with that crime (Sudnow 1965). Thus, some crimes which were considered serious by the state legislature were not so viewed by the court, because these offenses did not typically display dangerous or professional criminal activity—for example, bookmaking, homosexuality, mairjuana, pills, and other victimless crimes. One judge explained:

> Although the type of punishment legally defines a "felony," in actual fact—because "felony" carries with it other implications—an offense may be called a "felony" for reasons other than punishment. For example, bookmaking. Now, that crime used to be a city ordinance, a misdemeanor. But a police officer is only allowed to arrest on a misdemeanor charge if he witnesses the offense. But, of course, bookmaking goes on behind closed doors, so the officers weren't able to sustain their charges. When bookmaking is made a felony, then the cops can come in and charge for an offense which they didn't witness. *Bookmaking always gets a misdemeanor sentence, though.*

> Another example of this is these pill cases. They were made felonies just a few years ago. It was a clear example of the legislature panicking. The legislature thinks that the answer to all crime is to simply increase the punishment. Now that's absurd. Punishment is not going to solve the problem of pills. *I've never seen one pill case go to the state prison* [emphasis added].

In addition to prior record and offense, other factors were said to influence the sentence imposed: circumstances of the offense, personal characteristics of the defendant, the method of case disposition, and the defendant's admission of guilt to the probation officer. Judges acknowledged the importance of the circumstances of an offense, noting that sentences varied according to the amount of money or goods involved in a theft, whether injuries occurred in a robbery, the amount of drugs involved in a possession or sale case, and the identity and reputation of the victim. Judges also considered the age and background of an offender, looking at such factors as employment, education, and family background.

It is difficult to say exactly how race of the defendant influenced sentencing.[6] Black and Mexican-American defendants were less likely than Anglo-American defendants to have attributes of steady employment, education, and a clean record—all of which were advantages in sentencing. On the other hand, some judges had a double standard in sentencing and were more lenient with minority-group defendants. A P.D. characterized the judge he worked before:

> He's got the typical "white man's burden" attitude—which is the greatest for my clients. He's a racist. That's good for my clients because he's so loaded with guilt. He'll do anything he can to try and "help" these defendants [blacks and Mexican-Americans].

The only statistical data available on race and sentencing in Los Angeles was reported in Greenwood and associates (1976:57) for a sample of 2,617 burglary and robbery offenders in 1970. They found that, controlling for offense and prior record, Anglo-American defendants received felony sentences (rather than misdemeanor ones) about 5 percent more frequently than blacks and roughly 4 percent more than Mexican-Americans.

Another factor which may influence sentencing is the method of case disposition. The conventional wisdom in the criminal justice literature suggests a sharp difference in sentencing according to whether a defendant is convicted by a guilty plea or by trial, with lighter penalties going to those convicted by pleas (*Yale Law Journal* 1956; Vetri 1964; Enker 1967; Newman 1966; Neubauer 1974). For instance, when Neubauer asked attorneys in "Prairie City" if defendants there received a harsher penalty after conviction by jury trial, one defense attorney replied there was no question: "An unwritten rule of practice here is that if you go on trial and lose, there will be a harsher penalty" (1974:229).

Interestingly, my interviews with attorneys revealed *no* such definite "unwritten rule" or shared perception of sentencing practices in Los Angeles. Indeed, many Los Angeles attorneys saw *no* difference in sentencing for defendants convicted by trial or by plea in the superior court. Others described the practice in Los Angeles as one in which defendants convicted without a full trial were usually assured of a lenient sentence because of discussion with the judge in chambers; but defendants convicted by trial took risks on sentencing according to the results of the probation report, the facts which emerged during trial, and the more serious charge which might result from conviction by trial. As one P.D. said, "Judges in chambers will tell counsel, . . . 'This is what I'll give you if you plead now. After trial, I don't know what I'll do.'" After conviction by trial the sentencing risks generally involved a more severe penalty, but the opposite also occurred. As one P.D. explained:

> I've seen cases where the judge will sentence more *leniently* after a jury trial than he would have on a [nontrial] disposition. During the trial the judge may buy part of the defense's argument . . . and he takes that into consideration in sentencing. So he goes easier on the defendant after trial than he would have on disposition.

The sentencing risks of trial depended in part on the seriousness of the case. In "light" cases (minor offenses with defendants who had little or no record) defendants generally received the same sentence regardless of the method of case disposition. But defendants in "serious" cases were more likely to receive a harsher sentence with conviction by trial than with conviction by plea, especially because of differences in the final charge. In "serious" cases involving mandatory felonies and/or defendants with prior felony convictions, the judge was often restricted by statute from granting a misdemeanor sentence or probation if the defendant was convicted as charged. In a bargained disposition to a lesser charge (or if the D.A. agreed to offer no evidence on prior convictions—that is, "to strike the priors") then the judge would be able *and* more willing to use his discretion for a lenient sentence. One D.A. commented that judges did not penalize in sentencing defendants who have been convicted at trial, but with the following qualification:

> What often happens, though, is that by going to trial he [the defendant] gets convicted of a lot more serious charge than if he had taken a disposition to a lesser charge. Like we told them in that . . . case this morning: robbery conviction with a finding of "armed" would mean state prison. In [nontrial] disposition, the judge is saying the defendant will get something less for pleading guilty. But if the case goes to trial, then the judge is no longer bound by any earlier conditions. . . . A plea bargain may involve a different charge than the charge at trial; that's why the sentences would be different.

The effect of a defendant's plea on his sentence was also influenced by the reaction of the probation officer to the defendant's denial or admission of guilt. As one judge noted, the defendant who pleads guilty may "get a better probation report" because of the "remorse and contriteness" shown in conversations with the probation officer. A senior probation officer explained how a defendant's denial of guilt was considered in the probation officers' recommendations on sentencing:

> We have to assume over here that the guy did it. So when a defendant denies guilt, then we take that into consideration in our evaluation. But we go on other factors than just his attitude on guilt. For instance, he may in *fact* be innocent—I'm prepared to say that there may be error in the conviction process. Or, in a child molestation case, the defendant may be too ashamed of the offense to admit his guilt. Or, maybe he just has a mental block against admitting guilt. Among blacks, it's strongly felt for some that you don't cop out to the Man.
>
> So if he denies his guilt, that doesn't automatically preclude probation. But it is a factor in our evaluation. I did an informal survey of about half of the [probation] office here: only two out of the twenty-five deputy probation officers that I asked said that the defendant's denial

of guilt would *preclude* a recommendation of probation. All of the rest said that it would be a factor, but just one factor among many. Also, those two officers were new to the office [emphasis added].

Thus, as reported by participants in the Los Angeles court, sentences in "light" cases were generally not affected by the type of disposition method, while sentences in "serious" cases might be affected, especially because of differences in the final charge on conviction by trial and/or because of the probation officer's report. I do not have the statistical data to verify this. Greenwood and associates (1976:41-46) present a slightly different view on the relationship between disposition method and severity of sentence, based upon countywide data in 1970. They argue that sentence severity in Los Angeles does increase from nontrial to trial dispositions, thus supporting the conventional wisdom "that the system extracts some greater price from those who force it to go through all of the steps of formal adjudication" (Greenwood and associates 1976:42). There are three main problems with the analysis of Greenwood and associates. First, their conclusion is based upon the sentencing of six groups of defendants with different combinations of offense and prior record; all of the cases used are "serious" ones, involving mandatory felonies and/or defendants with major or prior prison records. For these "serious" cases sentencing after a trial conviction might in fact be more severe than after conviction by guilty plea. Secondly, analysis of disposition method and sentencing should also consider cases in which the defendant was acquitted at trial. After all, an *acquittal* following a trial disposition is a possible outcome, just as is an increased sentence.

Finally, a crucial problem with their discussion is that they assume that the cases settled by trial are equivalent, for *sentencing* purposes, to the cases settled by plea bargaining. This assumption is faulty since, as I show in the following chapters, anticipation of sentencing has a definite effect on the *choice* of disposition method. Any statistical analysis of the relationship between disposition method and sentencing should control for a number of case and defendant characteristics which might influence sentencing (for example, counts and charges of offense, and age, race, and prior record of defendant). Two recent studies, controlling for such factors, found that method of case disposition *per se* had little or no effect on sentence severity (Eisenstein and Jacob 1977; Wildhorn and associates 1976).[7]

One last factor influencing sentencing in Los Angeles was the individual variation among the twenty-six trial judges in the central district. While prior record and the offense type were important as general determinants of the sentence, a key factor was of course the individual judge himself. A few judges were perceived as particularly severe in sentencing. Defense attorneys would jokingly refer to these judges with "state prison" prefixed to their names, as "State Prison Jordan" or "Old State Prison Brown." Then there were a few judges who were perceived as exceptionally lenient, as one judge who was described by a D.A. as "Santa Claus—he gives you whatever you want." Another judge was characterized this way by a prosecutor: "Let me put it to you this way about Judge Greene: you can't *buy* in Chicago what Greene gives away for nothing!" Greenwood and associates (1976:158-159), in their statistical analysis of sentencing in Los Angeles, also reported large disparities among individual judges in sentence severity.

Summary

The D.A.s, P.D.s, and "regular" private defense attorneys in the criminal courts downtown know this general pattern of sentencing and they know how different kinds of cases are likely to fit into this pattern. Given the offense charged and the defendant's prior record, attorneys can roughly predict the sentence the defendant would receive. Given additional information on the facts and circumstances of the offense, on the defendant's background (age, family, employment, and so on), and on the individual sentencing judge or on alternative judges in short cause, they can predict the sentence with more certainty. All of this information on sentencing provides the basis for categorizing cases according to their seriousness—that is, according to the chances of a severe sentence on conviction. Although seriousness is a continuum, attorneys use dichotomous categories of "serious" and "light" to describe cases. Hence, cases are characterized as "serious" if there is a high chance of a severe sentence (for example, state prison or mental hygiene) or "light" if there is no real chance of prison and a high chance of probation.

There are two attributes by which cases are routinely identified as "serious." First, a mandatory felony offense creates a presumption of seriousness because lenient sentences are less common on these offenses. More specifically, those mandatory felony offenses which *typically* receive severe sentences are generally described as "serious." This includes homicide, robbery, kidnapping, opiates, forcible rape, and lewd acts with child. Second, a bad criminal record for a defendant (particularly a prior felony conviction) indicates that his case is "serious" regardless of his charged offense.

This routine identification of "serious" cases based only upon charged offense and prior record determines some of the snap decisions made about cases—particularly those organizational decisions assigning cases to individual P.D.s or D.A.s. Then, as individual attorneys investigate their cases and learn the specific facts and circumstances involved, they refine their sentence predictions and their categorizations. For example, what was thought to be a "serious" case may, on investigation, become a "light" one, as perceived by the defense attorney or the prosecutor. Note that this process of categorization goes on with individual D.A.s and defense attorneys (and, to an extent, with judges as well) before bargaining and/or trial begins. Convergence or divergence of prosecution and defense predictions of sentencing severity is a key factor in the process of case disposition (as will be shown in the following chapters). Note, too, that as attorneys begin the process of case disposition, including negotiations over the charge and chamberizing with the judge over the sentence, they are no longer predicting sentence severity, but instead are helping to shape the final sentence.

This framework of categorization of cases is similar to that suggested by Emerson (1969) in his ethnographic study of a juvenile court. Emerson found that juvenile court staff routinely sort cases into those which present real "trouble" and those which do not; the "trouble" case requires special handling to work out an appropriate disposition. The "serious" case in the adult court is like Emerson's "trouble" case; it, too, demands special attention in developing pretrial strategies and in plea bargaining. The cultural perspective of the adult court (unlike the juvenile court) also emphasizes the strength or weakness of the prosecution's case in the process of case disposition.

Strength of the Prosecution's Case

Defense and prosecuting attorneys categorize cases on the basis of the strength of the prosecution's case, in addition to categorizing according to seriousness. Strength reflects a prediction by attorneys of conviction or acquittal—a prediction which is based upon evaluation of the amount and type of evidence in view of perceived judge and jury behavior on the issue of reasonable doubt. The D.A.s evaluate their evidence against the defendant and characterize cases as "dead bang" where there is a very high chance of conviction. Weaker cases are either those where there is a chance of acquittal on the original charge but conviction on a lesser charge, or those with a chance of complete acquittal. Defense attorneys also evaluate cases as to the likelihood of conviction or acquittal. In making their predictions, defense attorneys have the benefit of knowing witnesses and evidence for the defense, as well as knowing much of the prosecution's case. Pretrial discovery rules are more favorable to defense than to the prosecution. Also, both parties have copies of the transcript of the preliminary hearing—at that hearing, crucial evidence and testimony for the prosecution are presented, but evidence is seldom introduced by defense. Thus defense attorneys, in predicting a high chance of conviction, refer to cases as "dead bang" if the D.A. has strong evidence against the defendant *and* if there is no credible or consistent explanation by the defendant for innocence. Weaker cases or, as defense attorneys sometimes described them, "reasonable doubt" cases are those with limited or conflicting evidence against the defendant and some plausible defense.

On the basis of the terminology of the attorneys and their evaluations of different cases according to the chances of conviction, three kinds of cases can be distinguished: "dead bang" cases—those with a very high chance of conviction as charged—and two kinds of "reasonable doubt" cases. In one type of "reasonable doubt" case, the doubt centers on the degree of the defendant's involvement in the crime or on the gravity of the offense; defense attorneys consider these cases to be "overfiled," and while there is a chance of acquittal on the original charge, there is a high likelihood of conviction on a lesser offense. In the other type of "reasonable doubt" case, the doubt stems from insufficient evidence either clearly to connect the defendant with the crime or to prove that any crime has been committed; in these cases, there is a good chance of complete acquittal.

Few cases in court are perceived by attorneys to be pure "reasonable doubt" cases, that is, cases with a good chance of a complete acquittal. The majority are "dead bang" or "overfiled reasonable doubt" cases. As one P.D. commented,

> The fact is that the doctrine of reasonable doubt is not useful anymore. In most cases, there's hardly any doubt at all. In fact, most of the cases we win at trial are because of sloppy prosecution.

Another P.D. made the same point: "Most of the cases we get are pretty hopeless—really not much chance of an acquittal." A private defense attorney similarly noted:

> Most of these guys are guilty. The police don't just go out arresting people and saying, "You're a burglar. You're a thief." That's not the way it is. From a defense lawyer like me, you might expect me to say there are a lot of innocent people being prosecuted. But that's not so. It happens, sure, but not very often.

Certain types of offenses typically have a greater or lesser chance of conviction because of the nature of evidence and testimony involved. The prosecution's case is strongest where physical evidence is involved, such as fingerprints or contraband found in possession of the defendant. Thus, many of the narcotics cases are "dead bang"; the best chance for defense is to obtain a dismissal following a successful search and seizure challenge, but it is difficult to obtain an acquittal once the evidence has been admitted. Heroin cases are particularly strong for the prosecution, not only because of the physical evidence, but also because heroin defendants frequently have criminal records which hurt their credibility as witnesses if they take the stand in trial. Marijuana defendants fare better before juries because some jurors are reluctant to convict on this offense when the defendant is young, with no record, and only a small quantity of marijuana is involved.

Some theft cases are also "dead bang"—where defendants have been caught in possession of the stolen goods. Forgery and bad checks cases are typically strong for the prosecution because the physical papers can be presented as evidence, with the handwriting verified by an expert. The prosecution also has strong cases where the defendant has been caught at the scene of the crime (for example, inside a store, having set off the burglar alarm) or where the police obtained a confession from the defendant.

Cases which are more likely to be considered "overfiled reasonable doubt" are those where the defendant is charged in the first degree, yet there is strong evidence only to convict of second degree. For example, a P.D. said,

> On murder cases, there may be reasonable doubt on first degree, but they're definitely gonna get him on second degree or manslaughter. It's the same with first degree burlgary or robbery.

Charges of "attempt" to do an illegal act also fall into this category—for example, "attempted burglary" or "assault with intent to commit rape." It is likely that the defendant will be convicted, for example, of trespass or simple assault, but it is harder for the prosecutor to prove the necessary intent. Another offense which is commonly perceived as "overfiled reasonable doubt" is grand theft auto. Defendants apprehended with a stolen vehicle are typically charged with both grand theft auto and felony joy riding (driving without consent).[8] But it is often difficult for the D.A. to prove that the defendant was actually the one who stole the car; convictions are more often obtained for the joy riding offense.

Cases which present real questions of guilt or innocence with a good chance of a complete acquittal are typically "just plain factual disputes," in the words of one defense attorney. The reputation and demeanor of witnesses (and defendant and victim) are important here to resolve the issues of credibility. Sex offenses (rape, sex perversion, and child molestation) have relatively good chances of acquittal because typically the conflict is between testimony of the defendant and the victim. In addition, it is a trying ordeal for victims to testify at trial and thus some are reluctant witnesses. Assault cases also present these factual disputes where the character and testimony of witnesses are particularly important. For example, assaults occurring in bars are relatively difficult to prove because of the condition of the witnesses. Similarly, assaults between family members or friends may involve victims who are reluctant to testify.

Table 3-3 shows the overall conviction rate by offense charged for all defendants initially charged with felonies in Los Angeles in 1970. In some cases defendants released without conviction were acquitted, while in others the charges were dismissed following a pretrial motion on evidence or "in the interests of justice." (Dismissals will be discussed further in chapter 4.) But to understand attorneys' predictions of conviction, it is also important to know the conviction rate, by offense, for cases settled by full trial. Table 3-3 also shows the conviction rate by offense charged, just for those cases settled by full court or jury trial (excluding submission on the transcript trials).

Table 3-3
**Overall Conviction Rate and Conviction Rate at Trial, by Offense Charged, for
Defendants Initially Charged with Felonies, Superior Court of Los Angeles
County, 1970**

Offense Charged	Number of Defendants	Overall Conviction Rate (%)	Number of Jury and Court Trials	Conviction Rate at Trial (%)
Homicide	398	79.4	144	76.3
Manslaughter, vehicle	69	92.8	7	100.0
Robbery	1,875	84.4	416	69.7
Assault	1,640	78.2	352	58.8
Burglary	4,670	87.9	488	70.5
Theft, except auto	2,092	75.1	234	54.7
Theft, auto	1,582	82.3	148	43.4
Forgery and checks	2,107	89.7	130	67.7
Rape, forcible	391	73.1	106	51.9
Other sex offenses	769	78.7	176	52.8
Total drug violations	13,824	78.5	1,235	65.1
Opiates	1,250	77.8	210	76.2
Marijuana	5,529	73.1	450	54.2
Dangerous drugs	6,851	82.8	561	59.3
Other drug violations	194	90.7	14	78.6
Deadly weapons	377	76.1	40	65.0
Drunk driving	371	95.2	32	90.6
Hit and run	109	91.8	15	73.3
Escape	146	94.5	4	50.0
Kidnapping	189	82.5	53	75.5
Bookmaking	701	79.9	35	57.1
Other	261	72.0	44	65.9
Total	31,571	81.5	3,659	64.6

Source: Administrative Offices of Superior Court of Los Angeles.

Defense and prosecuting attorneys examine the evidence in a case and compare it to that in similar cases. They evaluate the strength of the prosecution's case against perceived judge and jury behavior on reasonable doubt. On this basis, they categorize cases as "dead bang," "overfiled reasonable doubt," or "reasonable doubt" with a chance of complete acquittal, according to the likelihood of conviction. This categorization provides a basis for pretrial strategy, for plea bargaining, and for the choice of disposition method. Next I will show how these categories of seriousness and strength are used by participants in the process of case disposition.

4

Overview of the Court Process: From Arrest to Disposition

Criminal justice studies commonly depict the processing of felony cases in a flow chart. Figure 4-1 shows the flow of felony cases in Los Angeles County from arrest to conviction or acquittal. California state law can explain the various decision points and procedures available at each stage. But the law cannot explain how these procedures are used and interpreted by the regular court participants to produce the particular pattern of case processing found in Los Angeles. Instead we look to the informal rules, the shared values, and the cultural categories of the participants themselves to see how *they* define and organize the processing of felony cases. This chapter will describe the process shown in figure 4-1, with particular attention to the factors considered most important by participants in making pretrial decisions.

A major theme of this chapter can be stated simply at the outset. The pretrial process involves two kinds of "sorting" decisions. Participants make both of these decisions in anticipation of final case disposition, using the categorization of cases developed in the previous chapter. The first decision, based upon an evaluation of the strength of the evidence against the defendant, anticipates the likelihood of conviction or acquittal. This decision is the traditional screening decision made by prosecutors and lower court judges to weed out cases with weak or inadequate evidence. The second decision anticipates eventual punishment on conviction; this decision is made on the seriousness of the case, looking especially at the severity of the offense and the defendant's prior record. Note that, in a traditional legal view, issues of punishment should not be considered until *after* the defendant's conviction, but in fact such consideration occurs at the very beginning of the criminal process.

A second theme of the chapter points to the interdependence of decision-making in the criminal process. This interdependence accounts for the courts' remarkable self-adjusting capacity and seeming resistance to changes. That is, changing the decisions of one set of participants frequently leads to adaptations by others which effectively undermine the change. Sarat (1978:326) makes this point clearly when he compares the trial court process to an underinflated balloon: "Grab one end and the air moves to another. Change one component and problems simply reappear elsewhere."

The Decision to Prosecute

The first major screening point occurred between the arrest and the filing of felony charges. Of all adult felony arrests in Los Angeles in 1970, only 47

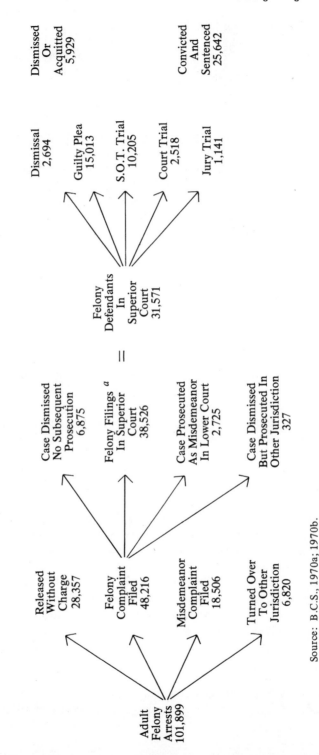

DECISION TO PROSECUTE

Adult Felony Arrests 101,899

Released Without Charge 28,357

Felony Complaint Filed 48,216

Misdemeanor Complaint Filed 18,506

Turned Over To Other Jurisdiction 6,820

PRELIMINARY HEARING

Case Dismissed No Subsequent Prosecution 6,875

Felony Filings ^{a} In Superior Court 38,526

Case Prosecuted As Misdemeanor In Lower Court 2,725

Case Dismissed But Prosecuted In Other Jurisdiction 327

=

Felony Defendants In Superior Court 31,571

SUPERIOR COURT DISPOSITION

Dismissal 2,694

Guilty Plea 15,013

S.O.T. Trial 10,205

Court Trial 2,518

Jury Trial 1,141

Dismissed Or Acquitted 5,929

Convicted And Sentenced 25,642

Source: B.C.S., 1970a; 1970b.

^{a}Number of filings includes multiple filings for a single defendant.

Figure 4-1. Disposition of Adult Felony Cases in Los Angeles County, 1970

percent were prosecuted as felonies, with 18 percent prosecuted as misdemeanors, 7 percent turned over to other jurisdictions, and 28 percent released
without charge (B.C.S. 1970b; see figure 4-1). I did not directly study the
decision to prosecute, but, because of the importance of this stage, I will briefly
summarize the process based upon other studies of Los Angeles.[1]

Following a felony arrest, a police investigating officer would examine the
case and then bring the police report and the defendant's prior record to a
complaint deputy in the D.A.'s office for the filing of charges. Although the
police screened some arrests, they generally waited until discussion with the
complaint deputy before actually dismissing or reducing charges. Then it was
common for the police officer to tell the D.A., as he gave him the case, that it
was a "reject" and no complaint would issue (Graham and Letwin 1971:644;
Greenwood and associates 1976:16). Thus, that less than one-half the felony
arrests resulted in the filing of felony charges did not necessarily show a high
degree of prosecutorial screening. Some of these cases represented, "instead, an
instance of police screening which is attributed to the prosecutor in order to
satisfy the bureaucratic needs of both organizations" (Graham and Letwin
1971:675). The police could blame the prosecutor for the release of so many
felony suspects, while the prosecutor could point to their high screening
standards to show they did not simply rubber-stamp police requests for
prosecution (Graham and Letwin 1971:675).

The countywide prosecutorial policy was that cases should be filed only
where there was a reasonable chance of conviction, but the operational meaning
and enforcement of that policy varied from one branch office to another.[2] In
the downtown office, filing standards tended to be fairly loose and informal,
"since the Complaints Unit is organizationally distinct from the Trials Unit and
the deputies involved in filing can never carry through the cases they begin"
(Greenwood and associates 1976:80). In branch offices without such specializa-
tion, D.A.s had an incentive for adhering to stricter filing standards since they
might eventually take to trial the cases they originally filed.

The prosecutor's decision to file a felony complaint was based primarily on
the strength of the case, but also on the desirability of felony prosecution. Cases
which might be prosecuted as misdemeanors "in the interests of justice," even
where there was sufficient evidence of a felony, involved offenses such as assault
between family members, statutory rape, bookmaking, and marijuana and pill
cases of small quantity. In May 1971, the D.A. formalized what had been
informal policy in some of the offices to allow these (and a few other) optional
felony offenses to be filed as misdemeanors rather than felonies.[3] The May 1971
policy directive also stated explicitly how the defendant's prior criminal record
could be considered by deputies in their decision to prosecute optional felony
offenses. Even before this directive, however, D.A.s had considered prior record
in some of their filing decisions. In a survey of Los Angeles prosecutors, the
Southern California Law Review (1969:529) found that almost three-quarters of
those questioned gave "great weight" or "some weight" to prior record in
determining whether to prosecute. At least one-third of the deputies surveyed

also stated that their filing decision was affected by the age, occupation, and intelligence of the defendant, the status of the victim, and public opinion (*Southern California Law Review* 1969:529).

That prosecutors in Los Angeles gave some consideration to the nature of the offense and the defendant's prior record in deciding which cases warranted felony treatment is consistent with studies of the decision to prosecute in other areas (Cole 1973; Carter 1974; Neubauer 1974). One job of the complaint deputy was to review the adequacy of the evidence. But at the same time, in choosing between misdemeanor and felony charges, the prosecutor was deciding "whether the accused deserves light or severe punishment" (Rosett and Cressey 1976:14).

A final aspect of the decision to prosecute is the problem of "overcharging" or "overfiling." That is, prosecutors may inflate the charges against a defendant (by bringing in multiple charges, or by filing an unrealistically high level of charge) simply to enhance their position in plea bargaining later.[4] Most attorneys in Los Angeles acknowledged that some overfiling occurred, but prosecutors denied that it was as common as defense attorneys suggested. Also, D.A.s differed in their own view of overfiling, and this affected their decisions on charges. One D.A. working in the trials division told me, "I think overfiling is unethical. I refused to do it when I worked in complaints." I asked if there was any pressure on him to overfile and he said:

> No, although I sure had some heated arguments with those around me. *The policy was to overfile.* The D.A.s upstairs [in the trials division] would say, *"Come on, give us something to work with!"* [emphasis added].

Another D.A. also explained, "Sure, there is overfiling in our office.... [It] does encourage [nontrial] disposition because compromises are more attractive." Thus, in choosing charges, prosecutors were making a cultural judgment, not just a legal judgment. That is, they evaluated a particular charge with a view to how that charge would be interpreted by others later in the process.

Municipal Court Arraignment and Preliminary Hearing

To commence felony prosecution, the prosecutor filed a complaint within forty-eight hours following the defendant's arrest. At that time, the defendant was arraigned in municipal court. The arraignment downtown was a rushed, extremely brief proceeding at which the municipal court judge read the charges, set bail, accepted applications for "O.R." (own recognizance) release, and assigned a date and courtroom for the preliminary hearing. Defendants were also informed, as a group, of their constitutional rights. The public defender was appointed to represent most defendants at this stage, since few private counsel came to the arraignment in municipal court.

In the central district the preliminary hearing was normally scheduled for two weeks after the arraignment. In the branch courts, where there was a much lighter caseload, there was a week or less before the preliminary. At the arraignment cases were assigned directly to one of the eleven divisions of the municipal court which handled preliminary hearings downtown. The deputy clerk in the arraignments division noted that the assignments were random except that the time for each hearing was estimated according to the type of offense involved in order to equalize the workload of the eleven divisions. The deputy clerk explained:

> We schedule nine hours of work per day to each division. That works out right since about 25 percent of the cases are continued at their preliminary. And we figure that a murder case takes all day. A 288a [case of sex perversion] takes thirty minutes; if a child is involved, then it's fifteen minutes more. Marijuana takes about twenty minutes for a prelim, although if there's a large amount involved, it'll take longer.

The average preliminary hearing in Los Angeles lasted about one-half hour (see also Graham and Letwin 1971:659; Greenwood and associates 1976:18). But, as indicated above, the length of the hearing seemed to depend on the type of offense and, even further, on the extent to which the offense was a typical one. The importance of the offense was related to the different defense strategies at the preliminary hearing, as discussed later in this section.

The preliminary hearing was almost always held in Los Angeles, in contrast to some courts in which a high percentage of defendants commonly waive this proceeding (see, for example, Casper 1972; Neubauer 1974; Eisenstein and Jacob 1977). At the hearing, the prosecutor would present evidence against the defendant, usually calling all of the important witnesses. The defense attorney then cross-examined the state's witnesses, but typically he did not present evidence for the defense. At the conclusion of the "prelim," the municipal court judge determined whether there was probable cause to believe the defendant guilty of the offense charged; if probable cause was found, the judge would hold the defendant to answer in superior court. In 1970, 14.2 percent of the felony complaints in Los Angeles were dismissed at the preliminary hearing with no subsequent prosecution; 5.4 percent were reduced to misdemeanors; and 0.7 percent were referred to other jurisdictions for prosecution (B.C.S. 1970a; see figure 4-1).[5]

That only one case in five was terminated prior to superior court indicates that the preliminary hearing in Los Angeles did not function as the major screening point that it did, for example, in Chicago or Brooklyn. In these cities, with virtually no advance prosecutorial screening, the vast majority of felony charges were dismissed or reduced at the preliminary hearing (Trammell 1969;

Oaks and Lehman 1968; Eisenstein and Jacob 1977). Similarly, in some California courts, plea bargaining was common at the preliminary hearing, with the frequent reduction of felony charges to misdemeanors (B.C.S. 1970a; and see Carter 1974). However, such reductions were not common in Los Angeles, and, consequently, "many matters which would be disposed of in municipal courts in other areas, reach the Los Angeles Superior Court where they are often disposed of by a misdemeanor sentence" (Judicial Council of California 1971:123).

Those few cases which were reduced to misdemeanors at the preliminary hearing typically involved minor offenses (such as bookmaking, bad checks, marijuana or pill cases) with a defendant of little or no criminal record. Consideration of the seriousness of the case was part of the D.A. policy in approving reductions and it also reflected P.D. policy on pleading in the lower courts. In the central district, the supervising P.D. (in the prelim division) generally discouraged pleas to reduced charges because of the lack of time for full investigation, the problem of rapport with clients from such early plea bargaining, and the risk of more severe sentencing from a municipal court judge than from a superior court judge later.[6]

The preliminary hearing in Los Angeles was particularly important for final case disposition since the transcript of the hearing often provided the basis for an abbreviated court trial (by S.O.T.—submission on the transcript). However, most Los Angeles defense attorneys did not present any defense at the prelim since municipal court judges generally did not decide issues of credibility or factual conflict.[7] "The defense should only try to weaken any prosecution testimony, not present anything new," as one P.D. said. Besides trying to weaken the D.A.'s case, defense attorneys sometimes used the preliminary hearing for discovery purposes.

An important strategic choice for the defense was involved here which necessitated anticipation of later disposition of the case. A P.D. described two preliminary hearing strategies as follows:

> The strategy for prelims is *to decide first whether the case will ultimately go to a full-blown trial or whether it will be settled by a plea or S.O.T.* If the case is going to go to full trial, then you use the prelim for discovery. You ask every possible question that you can and pursue vigorous cross-examination. That will give the fullest amount of information for the later trial deputy. If the case will probably *not* go to trial, that is, if it will be a plea or an S.O.T., then you want to say as little as possible. Because there you want an innocuous transcript. So just let the prosecution put on the bare bones of their case [emphasis added].

Where an attorney anticipated a nontrial disposition, he also might try to enter into the transcript mitigating evidence, that is, anything to justify or moderate the defendant's actions in the case. For example, a police officer would be asked, "Was the defendant cooperative at all times?" This defense question was not relevant for screening or for discovery, but it made the transcript look better for later sentencing. Similarly, a state's witness would not be vigorously interrogated for discovery if a nontrial disposition was expected, because that would load the record against the defendant.

Given that attorneys varied their preliminary hearing tactics depending on their guess as to how the case would ultimately be tried, it remains to determine on what basis this guess was made. Some defense attorneys, when asked about this, said simply that their strategy "depended on the case," or that "one just learns by experience." But others noted that the seriousness of a case as well as the strength of a case was considered in anticipating later disposition. A senior P.D. who supervised the training and actions of the other P.D.s doing preliminary hearings downtown explained how the seriousness of a case was a signal for a certain type of defense startegy at the preliminary hearing:

> *If a case is going to end in a heavy trial, then it's important that the preliminary hearing be used for discovery,* so that we can find out how much and what kind of evidence they have on the case. The prelim is not supposed to be a vehicle for discovery, but that is one of its big functions. . . . *On a very serious case, the discovery function is important.* You want to really cross-examine their witnesses under oath so in case they change their story at trial you can impeach them by their prelim testimony.

> *You don't use the prelim for discovery in all cases, though. In light cases you don't want to blow it up.* On a G.T.A. [auto theft] or a light burglary, if you go on asking too many questions, the case starts to look horrible. Or in an assault case, on cross-examination, she might start talking about the last three times this guy assaulted her—you know, the case can get blown up [emphasis added].

In the more "serious" cases, then, the preliminary was used for discovery in anticipation of a later trial, while, in the "light" cases, cross-examination at the preliminary was minimized in order to have a shorter, better-looking transcript for later nontrial disposition.

Because of the importance of the choice of preliminary hearing strategy, the P.D.'s office singled out certain cases for special attention. This meant that the P.D. assigned to the case had additional time for preparation. Similarly, the D.A.'s office allowed extra preparation time on its "specialed" cases. In both offices the most "serious" cases were likely to be "specialed," such as those involving murder, kidnapping, or aggravated robbery with injuries.

A final aspect of prelim decision-making involved the cases dismissed at the end of their preliminary hearings. In these cases, the prosecutor was free to refile a felony complaint on identical or different charges (P.C. Sec. 999). At the second preliminary hearing, the odds were that a new judge would hear the case since there were eleven different judges handling preliminary hearings downtown. If the D.A. refiled on a dismissed case, he could build a stronger record for the second hearing and hope that the new judge would be more favorable to the prosecution's case. The D.A.'s decision on refiling was largely determined by the strength and seriousness of the case. A D.A. working in the prelim division explained how he made this decision:

> *I look at the probability of conviction—how weak or strong the case is*—and weigh that against the public interest or cost to the community of prosecution. *A serious case is more likely to be refiled than a little one.* This case [a small theft case that had just been dismissed] I don't think will be refiled. It isn't very important. You see, in a small case like this one, the cost to the community is outweighed by the weak probability of conviction. But if it were a big case, then we'd refile. . . . *Prior record is also taken into consideration.* For example, on a G.T.A. [auto theft] where the guy's got a long history of G.T.A.s, *then even if it's a weak case, we refile.* There the weakness of the case is outweighed by the public interest in prosecuting the guy—you know, a habitual criminal [emphasis added].

Superior Court Arraignment

At the conclusion of the preliminary hearing, the magistrate set the date for arraignment in superior court for each defendant held to answer on a felony charge. In the central district the date was normally two weeks after the preliminary hearing, which was just within the statutory time limit of fifteen days. At arraignment in superior court, the D.A. would file an information, formally charging the defendant. In 1970, 98.9 percent of all felony defendants in Los Angeles were charged by means of an information, and only 1.1 percent were charged by certification or Grand Jury indictment (B.C.S. 1970a). Certification was used where the defendant had already pled guilty to a felony in municipal court, while the grand jury functioned as an alternate screening device to the preliminary hearing.

During 1970, all superior court arraignments in the central district were held in a master calender department, Dept. A, while after January 1971, cases were assigned directly to their trial departments for arraignment. The supervising judge, who presided over Dept. A, appointed the public defender to represent most indigent defendants; private attorneys were appointed in cases involving multiple defendants where the P.D. would represent only one, because of possible conflict of interest.

Once representation was established and the attorney and his client had conferred, the supervising judge informed the defendant of the charges and any allegations of prior felony convictions filed against him. The defendant then entered his plea. Only 3 percent of defendants in the central district in 1970 pled guilty at this arraignment (Greenwood and associates 1976:104). The percentage was small because of the volume of cases and lack of time for much investigation or negotiation in the master calendar department. Only two D.A.s and four P.D.s were assigned to Dept. A, handling hundreds of arraignments every week. Thus, the vast majority of defendants pled not guilty and were assigned a date and courtroom for trial. The trial date was usually seven or eight weeks away, which was just within the statutory time limit of sixty days between the filing of the information and trial.

As described in chapter 2, the supervising judge assigned cases to their respective trial departments with some consideration for the type of case involved. Defense attorneys had no say in the assignment of their cases except that they could request assignment to a short cause department. In requesting a short cause court, the defendant had to waive his right to jury trial, since only guilty pleas, or trials by submission on the transcript which would take less than one hour, were heard in the two short cause courts.[8] Where the defense knew there would be no pretrial motions and no full-blown trial, short cause had the advantages of a lenient judge for sentencing and a shorter wait for the trial date. Defendants assigned to short cause waited only two or three weeks before their cases were heard, in comparison to the seven or eight weeks before the trial date in other departments. The D.A.'s consent was necessary for short cause assignment; generally he agreed as long as the preliminary hearing transcript was fifty pages or less.

Defense attorneys considered several factors in requesting that a case go to short cause from the arraignment. A P.D. (a grade IV) who supervised the other P.D.s in Dept. A described these factors:

First, is there a search and seizure issue? The judges have limited short cause to trials only—no pretrial motions. So the case cannot involve a search and seizure issue for short cause.

Secondly, is it a simple case? It must be able to be heard in ten to twenty minutes. We consider less than the legally allotted time limit of one hour just to be sure.

Third, how serious a case is it? I won't let a defendant waive his right to jury trial in a serious case [emphasis added].

I asked the P.D. how he determined the seriousness of a case, and he replied,

You look at the charges, the facts of the offense, the defendant's age, his record. *If it's a light offense on a person with a bad record, then it's a serious case for him* [emphasis added].

When I asked, "What is a 'light offense'?" he answered,

Joy riding—a guy sees a car with keys in it and just drives it around the block. Or a small amount of dangerous drugs or marijuana. *It's not serious if it's likely to end up with probation or a small county jail sentence—that is, if it's likely to end up as a misdemeanor by P.C. Sec. 17.* Of course, if a guy has much of a prior record, then it won't be reduced to a misdemeanor—that's why the record is so important.

In conclusion, *we send a case to short cause if it's a simple case that will take a short time to try, that has no search and seizure issues, and that in all probability will be a misdemeanor if convicted* [emphasis added].

In addition to these factors, the P.D.s considered the strength of the prosecution's case and they recommended short cause assignment especially in "light, dead bang" cases. Another P.D. in Dept. A commented,

If the defense is weak and it's not a serious case, then we'll go to short cause for the lenient sentencing. But if we have a strong case, then we'll want to take it to trial.

A senior P.D. in Dept. A also noted that he and his colleagues constantly revised their specific criteria for sending cases to short cause:

We have our men [other P.D.s] in short cause for feedback on how the judges are ruling and the sentences they're giving out. When we have a backfire—that is, a ruling or sentence contrary to our expectations— then we reevaluate our cases and we don't send that kind of case to short cause anymore!

Case Disposition in Superior Court

Once a case was assigned to its courtroom for trial, then investigation and planning for final disposition would begin, since the case was finally in the hands of the D.A. and P.D. who would be responsible for trying it. Prior to courtroom assignment, different attorneys handled each stage of the proceedings, passing the defendant's case file from one deputy to another within the D.A. and P.D. offices. Both the D.A. and P.D. offices assigned their most experienced attorneys to the felony trials division and allocated to them the most time and investigative staff for case preparation. Because the court, D.A., and P.D. organizations were structured so that the major disposition decisions occurred in the trial departments, the private defense attorneys conformed to this pattern as well; they generally did not try to bargain their cases out before the assignment to a trial department. As one private defense attorney said, "You can't do anything before the trial is set."

Pretrial motions raised by defense were the first step toward final case disposition. These pretrial hearings were fairly common, occurring in about 20 percent of the cases,[9] and usually based on P.C. Sec. 995 or 1538.5. In a "995 motion," the defense attorney sought to quash the information (and thus have the case dismissed) because of insufficient evidence; this motion essentially called for review by a superior court judge of the magistrate's decision on probable cause at the preliminary hearing. In a "1538.5 motion," defense sought to suppress evidence which may have been illegally obtained; this motion was often argued in narcotics cases where, if successful, the cases were usually dismissed. Pretrial hearings in Los Angeles were generally independent of any plea negotiations and were quite adversarial in nature, in contrast, for example, to the compromise of due process procedures described by Blumberg (1967).

In 1970, 8.5 percent of the felonies in Los Angeles were dismissed in superior court; about one-half of these dismissals came from successful defense motions based upon P.C. Sec. 995 and 1538.5, and the remaining dismissals were made "in the interests of justice." For cases not dismissed, there were four alternative methods for final disposition. In 1970, 3.6 percent of felony defendants elected jury trial, 8.0 percent chose full court trial (without jury), 32.3 percent chose trial by "submission on the transcript," and 47.6 percent pled guilty (B.C.S. 1970a; see figure 4-1).

With a guilty plea, the defendant might plead guilty to the original offense charged, to a lesser offense, or to one of several offenses charged against him. The plea might be entered with a tacit understanding of the likely sentence or with an informal indication by the judge at to the probable sentence. Or, the judge might formally promise to give a certain sentence on the condition of a favorable probation report; in the event of an unfavorable report, the defendant would be allowed to withdraw his plea.

Trial by submission on the transcript involved an abbreviated trial (without jury) on the basis of the transcript of the preliminary hearing and, if desired, with additional evidence and testimony. Although authorized for all of California, S.O.T. trials rarely occurred in counties other than Los Angeles. Most S.O.T. trials in Los Angeles operated as "slow pleas" of guilty, and involved the same kinds of bargains as to charge and sentence as in a guilty plea. For example, the judge might commit himself (informally or formally) as to what the likely sentence would be if the defendant were found guilty; or there might be an agreement whereby the defendant would be convicted of a lesser charge in the S.O.T. trial. Conviction by S.O.T. had advantages over a guilty plea in that the defendant reserved his right to appeal and did not have to admit guilt (which was also a selling point for the defense attorney to his client).

The conviction rate in 1970 for S.O.T. trials was 81.0 percent, in comparison to a conviction rate of 69.8 percent for jury trials and 62.2 percent for court trials (B.C.S. 1970a). Although most S.O.T. trials were "slow pleas" of guilty, in some cases the S.O.T. proceeding was used for a negotiated acquittal, where the D.A. wanted to dismiss a case but felt he could not justify it to his superiors. The case was then submitted to the judge for acquittal. And in other cases, S.O.T. was a semiadversary proceeding where the defense conceded certain points in the case but wished to contest others; thus, argument was focused only on the issues in conflict, not on the entire case.

The extent to which negotiation (with a guilty plea or S.O.T.) centered on the reduction of charges, rather than on a sentence commitment, depended primarily on the offense involved. Table 4-1 shows the level of *charge* on conviction, by the offense charged, for all defendants convicted in 1970. Table 4-1 also shows the percent of defendants who received misdemeanor *sentences* (that is, the level of conviction) by offense charged.[10] For some offenses (for example, marijuana, dangerous drugs, bookmaking) there was very little actual charge reduction, although there was a high percentage of misdemeanor sentences. For other offenses (for example, assault, auto theft, other sex offenses) charges were frequently reduced (to a lesser felony or to a misdemeanor) to accompany misdemeanor sentences. But for still other offenses (for example, homicide, robbery) there was frequent reduction to a lesser felony charge, but still with a high percentage of felony sentences. These differences among offenses depended upon statutory prescriptions for sentencing, D.A. policy in approving charge reductions, and judicial sentencing patterns. The differences will be explained further in chapters 5 and 6.

During the interval between the defendant's not-guilty plea in Dept. A and the trial date in a specific courtroom, the defense attorney would investigate his client's case and discuss with him the alternative methods of disposition. Bargaining by defense with the D.A. usually did not occur until just before, or the morning of, the trial date. If a defense attorney thought that a nontrial disposition (guilty plea or S.O.T.) was appropriate, he would approach the D.A. with an offer. Since the prosecution normally had the position of strength, it was protocol for the defense attorney to go to the D.A. with the suggested nontrial disposition. One D.A. said that he would never approach a defense attorney with a deal because "then they'd think we had a weak case." Indeed, defense attorneys did think that way, as typified by the following P.D. comment:

> *Usually we approach the D.A. for a deal.* But if they have problems—like they can't find their witness—then they may come to us with an offer. But of course they would never tell you that their witness is missing—you've got to look at their offers very carefully. *You get to know their habits, so you know what it means for the D.A. to come in with an offer* [emphasis added].

The suggested nontrial disposition was generally based upon the defense attorney's perception of the strength and seriousness of the case. That is, the attorney determined his offer by a *realistic* estimate of the best outcome at adversary trial and the best sentence which his client was likely to obtain. If the

Table 4-1
Level of Convicted Charge and Level of Conviction, by Offense Charged, for Defendants Convicted and Sentenced in Superior Court of Los Angeles County, 1970

Offense Charged	Defendant Total	Level of Convicted Charge			Level of Conviction
		% Convicted of Felony as Charged	% Convicted of Lesser Felony Charge	% Convicted of Misdemeanor Charge	% Misdemeanor Sentence
Homicide	316	33.9	65.2	.9	3.5
Manslaughter, vehicle	64	81.3	0.0	18.8	53.1
Robbery	1,582	54.4	39.4	6.1	26.7
Assault	1,283	47.7	19.8	32.5	67.0
Burglary	4,104	65.6	21.2	13.2	56.7
Theft, except auto	1,571	70.5	14.5	15.0	63.3
Theft, auto	1,302	11.4	82.3	6.3	65.9
Forgery and checks	1,889	91.6	6.0	2.3	54.7
Rape, forcible	286	34.6	52.8	12.6	44.1
Other sex offenses	605	57.7	6.4	35.9	61.5
Total drug violations	10,858	86.5	9.1	4.4	63.3
Opiates	972	69.7	25.6	4.7	16.3
Marijuana	4,039	85.4	8.3	6.2	72.3
Dangerous drugs	5,671	90.1	6.8	3.1	64.9
Other drug violations	176	91.5	6.3	2.3	63.1
Deadly weapons	287	85.7	4.5	9.8	77.7
Drunk driving	353	80.2	0.0	19.8	64.3
Hit and run	100	88.0	1.0	11.0	67.0
Escape	138	98.6	0.0	1.4	94.2
Kidnapping	156	12.2	81.4	6.4	21.8
Bookmaking	560	98.6	0.0	1.4	93.0
Other	188	62.2	20.7	17.0	45.7
Total	25,642	72.5	18.4	9.1	59.3

Source: Administrative Offices of Superior Court of Los Angeles.

D.A.'s categorization of the case *converged* with that of the defense attorney, then they did not really negotiate; instead, they jointly sought to implement the agreed-upon disposition. If implementation depended upon charge reduction, then the D.A. had to secure permission from his superiors before accepting a plea to a lesser charge. Without such permission, the D.A. and the defense attorney might approach the judge for an S.O.T. trial with conviction on the lesser charge. If implementation depended upon a sentence indication or promise, then the defense attorney would try to have the case heard by a judge who would be favorable in sentencing (an issue to be discussed in more detail below).

On the other hand, if the D.A.'s perceptions and expectations about the case did *not* converge with the defense attorney's, then the attorneys discussed the case to resolve their differences. The more divergent their individual categorizations, the more likely that explicit bargaining would occur. If, even after bargaining, they still could not agree, the defense attorney might try to persuade a judge to go along with the deal (over the objections of the D.A.), or he might stall the disposition (hoping the D.A. would change his mind), or he might decide upon full adversary trial.

Whatever agreement (or nonagreement) that the attorneys arrived at, the defense attorney still had to return to his client for the final decision on disposition. Defense attorneys varied as to how strongly they would encourage clients to accept their recommendation on case disposition. Likewise, defendants differed on how much they were willing to gamble by refusing to accept a bargained disposition. These issues, as well as other aspects of the defense attorney/client interaction will be discussed in chapter 7.

Many of the guilty pleas and S.O.T. dispositions depended upon the judge's agreement to a particular range of sentence or to a misdemeanor level of conviction. Thus, a key question for a defense attorney was how the judge would exercise his discretion in sentencing. Defense attorneys tried to have their cases "disposed of" (settled without trial) by judges whose sentencing behavior they could fairly accurately predict, or by judges who would "chamberize," that is, who would indicate to defense counsel in chambers what the likely sentence would be. If the judge assigned to hear the case did not appear favorable to his client, the defense attorney chose among several strategies to have the case transferred to another judge.

The most common method of transferring a case (and the only one sanctioned by the court) was to go to one of the two short cause courts. Judges who would chamberize and who were perceived to be lenient sentencers were generally assigned to the short cause departments, thus facilitating nontrial dispositions. The D.A.'s consent to a transfer to short cause was sometimes part of a bargained disposition, since prosecutors knew that a particularly lenient sentence might result from going before a short cause judge.

A defense attorney could also transfer a case out of a courtroom to another (although he could not specify which court he would be sent to) by means of a 995 motion or an affidavit of prejudice filed against the judge. One judge explained how these procedures were used for judge-shopping:

> Judge-shopping is not supposed to happen here, but it does. For example, on the day of trial, a defense attorney files a 995 motion to have the case dismissed for insufficient evidence. The judge rules on that and if it's denied, then the attorney can ask for a new judge for trial since that judge is prejudiced by hearing the motion. So the case gets sent to a different court.

> Affidavits are also used for judge-shopping. An affidavit is only supposed to be used for cases of actual prejudice. But the judge isn't prejudiced at all—it's just that he might not be a very good judge, so the defense wants a different one. Only one affidavit is allowed for each case. Once it is exhausted, it can't be used again.

Finally, a defense attorney could usually have his case transferred to another courtroom by asking for a jury trial. The court coordinator then sent the case to whatever courtroom was available and open for trial. In part, defense request for jury trial could be a threat to the D.A. to persuade him to accept a plea bargain. But more often, it was simply a strategy to have the case heard by a different judge. As one P.D. explained to me:

> You can ask for a jury trial. That pressures the D.A. and he might come around then. . . . Or, once you're in the new trial department, you might get a new D.A. or you talk to the judge. They might be more reasonable in the new court, so you can dispose of it [settle without trial] there.

One way to transfer to a *particular* court was for defense to tell the court coordinator that he would waive jury before a certain judge (or judges) who was (were) perceived to be favorable to defense. In the interest of easing congestion in the courts, the coordinator would send the case to one of those judges. Once before the new judge, the defense attorney might be able to arrange a nontrial disposition, or he might still have a full trial. For example, a P.D. transferred a robbery case to Dept. H for a court trial. I asked how the case happened to come to Dept. H, and the P.D. said:

> It's a little game we play. We were all tied up in our court. So I announced "ready for jury trial." My man [defendant] didn't want jury, but I said that so that I wouldn't get sent out to some judge that's only open for court trial a few hours in the afternoon. Like they'd send me to [Judge] Rivers. He's always open, but he finds everybody guilty. I didn't want him. Or Judge Bard is always open but he's such an asshole, I always affidavit him. . . . So I played the game: I told the

court coordinator that I had a jury trial, but that we'd waive jury before Judge Stacey [in Dept. H]. So here we are.

Thus, the ability of defense to "shop" for a favorable judge expanded the options for adversary trial as well as the options for nontrial disposition.

Case Categorization and Disposition Method

The discussion above presents a brief overview of the process of case disposition in Los Angeles. The next two chapters will show the dynamics of the process with descriptions of numerous case dispositions. However, before proceeding to the case materials, I will summarize very generally how case categorization was related to disposition method. Defense and prosecuting attorneys each investigated their cases and estimated the chance of conviction and the probable sentence on conviction. In discussions of case disposition, the attorneys then compared their evaluations of strength and seriousness, and perhaps bargained to resolve their different evaluations. These discussions reflected a fine-tuning of case categorization, with attorneys in felony trials using fairly detailed information on evidence, possible testimony from witnesses, defendant's background for sentencing, and so forth. Attorneys earlier in the process, pressed for time and having very limited information, made only rough judgments of case evaluation. The earlier case evaluations (for example, in preliminary hearings) were also based on anticipated, or predicted, outcomes. In contrast, in these final plea negotiations, the attorneys' expectations would very likely determine the case outcome. If defense and prosecuting attorneys succeeded in their bargaining, a *tentative* case disposition was the particular charge and range of sentence where their expectations of conviction and sentence converged; the *final* disposition reflected agreement of the defendant and a judge to the disposition arranged by the attorneys.

There were two situations in which expectations of defense and prosecuting attorney were most likely to be divergent and in which bargaining had the least chance of success. Typically a full adversary trial would then be chosen to settle the case. A D.A. summarized these two situations as follows:

> *The weaker a case is, from our standpoint, the more likely it will be tried.* There the defendant thinks he can walk away from it. Rather than take a [bargained] disposition, he'll try to beat it altogether. Another kind of case that's often tried is the really hopeless case. There we have *an overwhelmingly strong case and it's a bad, very serious case where the defendant has a long record.* So he'll go to state prison anyway. He's got nothing to lose by trying it [emphasis added].

In terms of the framework of case categorization developed in chapter 3, those cases which were most likely to be settled by full trial were: (1) "reasonable doubt" cases where the defendant had a chance of complete acquittal and (2) "serious, dead bang" cases where the D.A. insisted on a state prison sentence. The ethnographic data to support this will be presented in the following chapters while some simple statistical analysis is discussed below.

There was a strong relationship between disposition method and type of offense. Table 4-2 shows disposition by offense for all defendants charged with felonies in 1970. Table 4-3 then gives a rank ordering of offense types by the frequency of adversary trial. While 11.6 percent of the *total* felony dispositions were resolved by adversary trial, 36.1 percent of the homicides, 28 percent of the kidnappings, and 27.1 percent of the forcible rapes were settled by full court or jury trial, as compared with only 8.6 percent of the drunk driving, 8.2 percent of the marijuana and dangerous drug cases, 6.2 percent of the forgeries, and 5.0 percent of the bookmaking cases.

Let us consider two explanations for this relationship: one relates to expected acquittal at trial and the other relates to expected severity of punishment. The first hypothesis was suggested by Kalven and Zeisel (1971). They found a negative correlation between the frequency of guilty pleas and the odds on acquittal at trial for fifteen major crimes. They concluded that a major

Table 4-2
Disposition of Felony Defendants in Los Angeles Superior Court, by Offense Charged, 1970

Offense Charged	Total Defendants	Jury Trial	Court Trial	Trial by S.O.T.	Guilty Plea	Dismissal
Homicide	398	91	53	80	147	27
Manslaughter, vehicle	69	3	4	15	45	2
Robbery	1,875	191	225	470	881	108
Assault	1,640	113	239	509	658	121
Burglary	4,670	180	308	1,486	2,456	240
Theft, except auto	2,093	51	183	692	939	227
Theft, auto	1,582	33	115	551	791	92
Forgery and checks	2,107	36	94	532	1,371	74
Rape, forcible	391	36	70	90	160	35
Other sex offenses	769	66	110	249	296	48
Total drug violation	13,824	266	969	4,900	6,141	1,548
Opiates	1,250	60	150	395	478	167
Marijuana	5,529	87	363	1,991	2,293	795
Dangerous drugs	6,851	116	445	2,451	3,259	580
Other drug violations	194	3	11	63	111	6
Deadly weapons	377	4	36	137	156	44
Drunk driving	371	10	22	100	231	8
Hit and run	109	6	9	30	62	2
Escape	146	0	4	22	118	2
Kidnapping	189	28	25	44	79	13
Bookmaking	701	4	31	235	374	57
Other	261	23	21	63	108	46
Total	31,571	1,141	2,518	10,205	15,013	2,694

Source: Administrative Offices of Superior Court of Los Angeles.

Table 4-3

Rank Ordering of Offenses Charged against Felony Defendants in Los
Angeles Superior Court, by Frequency of Trial Disposition, 1970

Offense Charged	Total Defendants	Defendants Disposed of by Full Court or Jury Trial (excludes S.O.T.)		
		Total %	% Court	% Jury
Homicide	398	36.1	13.3	22.8
Kidnapping	189	28.0	13.2	14.8
Rape, forcible	391	27.1	17.9	9.2
Other sex offenses	769	22.9	14.3	8.6
Robbery	1,875	22.2	12.0	10.2
Assault	1,640	21.5	14.6	6.9
Opiates	1,250	16.8	12.0	4.3
Other	261	16.8	8.0	8.8
Hit and run	109	13.7	8.2	5.5
Theft, except auto	2,092	11.1	8.7	2.4
Deadly weapons	377	10.6	9.5	1.1
Burglary	4,670	10.4	6.6	3.8
Manslaughter, vehicle	69	10.1	5.8	4.3
Theft, auto	1,582	9.4	7.3	2.1
Drunk driving	371	8.6	5.9	2.7
Marijuana	5,529	8.2	6.6	1.6
Dangerous drugs	6,851	8.2	6.5	1.7
Other drug violations	194	7.2	5.7	1.5
Forgery and checks	2,107	6.2	4.5	1.7
Bookmaking	701	5.0	4.4	.6
Escape	146	2.7	2.7	—
Total	31,571	11.6	8.0	3.6

Source: Computed by author based on data from Administrative Offices of Superior Court
of Los Angeles.

factor affecting the defendant's decision to plead guilty was "the over-all
likelihood of his being acquitted if he elects to stand trial" (Kalven and Zeisel
1971:22). However, this hypothesis is not strongly supported by data on
disposition by offense in Los Angeles. Table 4-4 compares the frequency of trial
dispositions with the conviction rate at trial for fourteen offenses.[11] The rank
order correlation coefficient between frequency of trial and conviction rate at
trial was −.30, indicating a not very strong relationship (not significant at the
.05 level). Note that we have suggested that "reasonable doubt" cases were likely
to be settled by trial, but perhaps expectations of acquittal varied more with
individual cases than they did by *offense* types.

A second explanation for the relationship between frequency of trial and
offense type involves expected severity of punishment. Table 4-4 compares the
frequency of trial with the proportion of severe sentences, for fourteen offenses,
where severity is measured by the percentage of defendants sentenced to state
prison or to the Department of Mental Hygiene. The rank order correlation

Table 4-4
Comparison of Adversary Trial, Conviction Rate at Trial, and Sentence Severity, by Offense Charged, Los Angeles Superior Court, 1970

Offense Charged	*Proportion of Adversary Trial*		*Conviction Rate at Trial*[a]		*Proportion of Severe Sentences*[b]	
	Percent	*Rank*	*Percent*	*Rank*	*Percent*	*Rank*
Homicide	36.1	1	76.3	1	56.3	1
Kidnapping	28.0	2	75.5	3	39.7	2
Rape, forcible	27.1	3	51.9	14	20.6	4
Other sex offenses	22.9	4	52.8	13	15.0	5
Robbery	22.2	5	69.7	5	24.5	3
Assault	21.5	6	58.8	9	6.8	7
Opiates	16.8	7	76.2	2	13.8	6
Theft, except auto	11.1	8	54.7	10	3.2	10
Deadly weapons	10.6	9	65.0	8	2.8	12
Burglary	10.4	10	70.5	4	6.1	8
Auto theft	9.4	11	53.4	12	3.1	11
Marijuana	8.2	12	54.2	11	.8	14
Dangerous drugs	8.2	13	69.3	6	1.7	13
Forgery and checks	6.2	14	67.7	7	5.3	9

Source: Computed by author based on data from Administrative Offices of Superior Court of Los Angeles.

[a]"Trial" means full court and jury trial combined, excluding S.O.T. trials.

[b]Sentence severity is measured by the percentage of defendants sentenced to state prison or Department of Mental Hygiene.

coefficient between frequency of trial and sentence severity was .88 (significant at the .01 level), indicating a very strong relationship. In terms of our categorization of cases this high correlation coefficient tends to support the proposition that the most "serious" cases (that is, those with a high chance of severe sentence) were the most difficult to settle by bargaining, and hence the most likely to be settled by adversary trial. On the other hand the relationship could also mean that cases which were resolved by trial received more severe sentences than those resolved without trial. Which way does the arrow of causality go? My interview and observational data indicate that the choice of trial disposition was heavily dependent upon anticipated sentence severity. But I also found that, in some "serious" cases, sentencing following trial was more severe than it would have been following a bargained disposition (although this was generally not true in the "light" cases—see chapter 3). More detailed statistical analysis, based on individual cases rather than simply offense categories, would be useful here to test these interpretations.

The "seriousness" of a case is indicated by the defendant's prior criminal record as well as by the type of offense, since defendants with bad records were more likely to receive severe sentences. Greenwood and associates present data for Los Angeles which show that "as severity of prior record increases, there is some increase in the likelihood of a jury or court trial" (1976:40). While 14.1 percent of the defendants with prison records took their cases to trial, only 11.9 percent of defendants with major records, 10.9 percent of defendants with minor records, and 9.5 percent of defendants with no record had trial dispositions (Greenwood and associates 1976:42). Again this is in comparison to 11.6 percent of *all* dispositions which were by full trial in 1970. This variation can be explained by expectations of sentence severity, while it is contradicted by the hypothesized expectation of acquittal at trial. Defendants with longer criminal records were more likely to be *convicted* at court or jury trial than defendants with lesser records, and yet these defendants (with longer records) slightly more often *selected* court or jury trial (Greenwood and associates 1976:42). Thus there is some statistical evidence to show that seriousness of a case—as indicated by prior record and offense type—was related to the frequency of adversary trial disposition. The next two chapters will explain and illustrate how the features of seriousness and strength interacted to lead to trial or nontrial dispositions.

5

The Dynamics of Case Disposition: The "Light" Case

Once a felony case reached its trial department in superior court, the defense attorney had to decide whether to seek a plea bargain or go to trial. There was wide agreement among defense attorneys (both private and P.D.) on which cases "ought" to be tried and which "ought" to be settled without trial. This chapter and chapter 6 will describe the case disposition process from the perspective of this defense attorney norm on the choice of disposition methods. Chapter 7 will then discuss the variation among defense attorneys in the advice they gave to their clients, including a comparison of P.D.s and private attorneys. Chapter 7 will also consider aspects of the defense attorney/client relationship, and the variation among defendants in acceptance of their attorneys' recommendations on trial or plea bargain.

In preparation for final disposition, defense and prosecuting attorneys each investigated their cases, checking, for example, the arrest report made by police, the criminal record of the defendant, the preliminary hearing transcript, testimony of possible witnesses, any physical evidence, and other information pertinent to the case. To estimate the likelihood of conviction, attorneys evaluated the strengths and weaknesses of the evidence against perceived judge and jury behavior on the issue of reasonable doubt. At the same time, attorneys considered the sentencing alternatives and the defendant's background to predict the probable sentence if convicted. In their discussions of final disposition, defense attorneys and prosecutors compared evaluations of strength and seriousness, and they might bargain to seek agreement on a nontrial settlement. The defense attorney recommended to his client trial or negotiated disposition based upon his interaction with the prosecutor and his own evaluation of the case. Table 5-1 shows the general pattern of recommended disposition method according to the strength and seriousness of the case, and the convergence or divergence of defense attorney and prosecutor views on expected outcomes. The process accompanying the disposition of "light" cases is described here. The disposition process for "serious" cases is described in the following chapter.

In "light" cases there was no chance of a state prison sentence and a good chance of probation. The offenses involved were typically considered minor and the defendants had minimal criminal records. The D.A.s were seldom concerned with sentencing in "light" cases. Thus, any conflict between prosecutor and defense attorney tended to be over the likelihood of conviction rather than over the sentence to be imposed. In "dead bang" cases, agreement between the prosecutor and defense attorney on a nontrial disposition was usually reached

Table 5-1

Recommendations by Defense Attorneys on Method of Disposition as a Function of Strength of Prosecution's Case, Seriousness of Case, and Convergence of D.A. and Defense Attorney Views

| Strength of Prosecution's Case (Prediction of Conviction or Acquittal) | *Seriousness of Case (Prediction of Severity of Sentence)* | | |
| | | *"Serious" Case* | |
	"Light" Case	*If D.A. and Defense Attorney Views Converge*	*If D.A. and Defense Attorney Views Diverge*
"Dead bang" case	Negotiated disposition (implicit bargaining)	Negotiated disposition (explicit bargaining)	Trial
"Reasonable doubt"— chance of conviction on lesser charge	Negotiated disposition (implicit or explicit bargaining)	Negotiated disposition (explicit bargaining—convergence more likely here than above)	Trial
"Reasonable doubt"— chance of complete acquittal	Indeterminate	Negotiated disposition (explicit bargaining)	Indeterminate

with little conflict; the D.A. knew that he would get a conviction as charged, while the defense attorney knew that his client would probably get a misdemeanor sentence with no incarceration or time served. Most bargaining between the attorneys in these cases was implicit. That is, the attorneys operated on the basis of a shared understanding that predictably lenient treatment would accompany a nontrial disposition. This process contrasts with explicit plea negotiation in which there are proposals and counterproposals, with clear specification of the terms of the final agreement.[1]

In "light" cases with "reasonable doubt" on the degree of the crime or on the degree of the defendant's involvement, the disposition process was similar to that for the "light, dead bang" cases. That is, a nontrial disposition was usually arranged, with both attorneys knowing that conviction was likely on a lesser charge and that the defendant would receive a lenient sentence. Further, both attorneys knew the kinds of charge reductions and dismissals routinely permitted by D.A. office policies, as well as the ways to avoid these policies by enlisting the cooperation of the judge. Bargaining accompanying these dispositions was implicit or explicit according to how apparent the weaknesses were in the evidence, and according to D.A. policy for the offense involved. Certain particular offenses were routinely charged by the D.A.s at a higher level than the expected conviction; for these offenses, charge reduction was almost automatic and entailed little or no negotiation over specific facts in the case. However, for other offenses, charge reduction in a nontrial disposition depended upon particular circumstances in the case and might require explicit negotiation.

In "light" cases with "reasonable doubt" that the defendant was guilty of *any* offense, defense attorneys generally sought a complete acquittal. That, of course, presented maximal conflict with the prosecutor, who wanted a conviction no matter what the level of charge. If the prosecution's case was very weak and if the D.A. was perceived to be receptive, then the defense attorney might try to persuade the D.A. to dismiss the charge or to talk to the judge to arrange an S.O.T. trial for not guilty. If the defense attorney so approached the D.A., there would be explicit bargaining accompanying a nontrial disposition of acquittal (S.O.T. for not guilty) or dismissal. If the bargaining was not successful, then the defense attorney recommended full trial to obtain an acquittal. Or, the defense attorney might decide not to discuss the case with the D.A. beforehand, instead going directly to adversary trial. There were few or no sentencing risks in a trial of this type since the defendant's sentence even after conviction by trial would probably still be probation.

The "light" cases illustrating these various dispositions are organized below according to offense types since the offense itself was crucial for attorneys' perception of cases and for their disposition decisions. Regular court participants routinely made decisions according to whether a given case was a typical or "normal" one for the offense charged. Sudnow's (1965) concept of "normal crime," while developed to explain decision-making by public defenders, also applies to the decision-making of most private attorneys, D.A.s, and judges.

To illustrate the details of the disposition process for "light" cases, I will first discuss the offense category of marijuana possession. Then I will present case material for other typically "light" offenses: possession of dangerous drugs, bookmaking, homosexuality, forgery and bad checks, auto theft, burglary, and assault.

Possession of Marijuana

"Dead Bang" Cases

Possession of marijuana, a violation of Section 11530, Health and Safety Code, typically involved young defendants with little or no criminal record. The offense was an "optional felony"; that is, it was punishable by felony or misdemeanor sentence. The "dead bang" cases were settled by a guilty plea or an S.O.T. trial for guilty (slow plea). In the following case, the defendant was a young black woman who had been released on bail. The day of her trial, her attorney, a P.D., arranged with the D.A. to have the case transferred to a short cause court for a change of plea. The judge in the court where the case was originally assigned was known to dislike sentencing without a probation report and the P.D. wanted immediate sentencing. During recess the next morning in short cause, the two attorneys went into chambers to talk to the judge:

Judge: What have you got this morning?

P.D.: It's a marijuana case. Small quantity. My client is twenty-six, a mother of two children. She was tripping and got scared and called the police. She has no record at all.

Judge: What do you want to do?

P.D.: Do you want a probation report? We'd like immediate sentencing.

Judge: Not if it's her first offense. I'll give her summary probation, $100 fine, and make it a misdemeanor by Section 17 [Penal Code].

P.D.: I'd rather have her on formal probation than the fine. She doesn't have much money.

Judge: She's getting both. It's not either/or. I want her to realize just how much that marijuana cigarette costs.

The attorneys left the judge's chambers and the P.D. told his client what the judge had said. When the case was called, the P.D. announced that his client wished to change her plea of not guilty to guilty. The D.A. "took the waivers," that is, he asked the defendant a series of questions to ascertain that she understood the nature and consequences of the proceedings, that she waived her rights to jury trial, cross-examination of witnesses, and self-incrimination, and that no promises or threats had been made to induce the plea of guilty. The judge accepted the plea of guilty to possession of marijuana and the defense attorney requested immediate sentencing. The judge then declared the offense to be a misdemeanor by Section 17, and fined the defendant $100, with a sixty-day stay for payment.

In the next marijuana case, a private attorney similarly arranged with the D.A. to transfer the case to the same short cause courtroom for a change of plea. In this case, the marijuana charge was accompanied by a misdemeanor charge of resisting arrest. The D.A. had agreed to drop the misdemeanor in exchange for a guilty plea to the marijuana charge, with the understanding that the judge would make the marijuana offense a misdemeanor by sentence. The D.A.'s action reflected a standard D.A. office policy of dropping additional charges when there is a plea to one; for most cases, this was simply routine procedure and did not involve explicit bargaining. Before the case was called in court, the D.A. and the defense attorney spoke to the judge in chambers:

D.A.:   This is a marijuana case with one joint, with a [P.C. Sec.] 148 [resisting arrest]. The boy has no prior record at all. He's a student at the State University, a senior, and a star basketball player. We'll take a plea to the 11530 and drop the other charge. And we have no objections if you reduce it to a misdemeanor.

Judge: All right. $100 fine, summary probation, and he's to stay away from all drugs. And I'll make it a misdemeanor by Section 17.

Def. Atty.: Immediate sentencing, then?

Judge: Yes.

These two cases illustrate a common pattern for the disposition of "dead bang" marijuana cases. The defense and prosecuting attorneys assumed that, unless there was some unusual aspect to a case, the case would be "disposed of"—that is, settled by guilty plea or by S.O.T. The disposition was to the original (optional) felony as charged, usually with assurance from the judge that the "normal" lenient sentence and misdemeanor conviction level would be imposed. In talking to the judge, the attorneys simply established that the case was a typical or "normal" one. Important elements of the typical marijuana case included: minimal prior criminal record; small quantity of the drug; other mitigating information regarding the defendant (for example, "mother of two," university student and "star basketball player") and regarding the circumstances of the offense (for example, defendant called the police herself). It made no difference which attorney (defense or D.A.) described the case to the judge; usually the attorney who knew the judge better would do most of the talking in chambers.

There were several variations on the pattern of behavior described above. For example, not all defense attorneys would speak to the judge before disposition; some attorneys, who were quite familiar with the judge's sentencing habits, would not even bother with this one- or two-minute conversation in chambers. For example, one very experienced P.D. commented with pride, "I don't always chamberize. I'm not that insecure." In addition, not all judges would chamberize. If the defense attorney was fairly certain about the judge's sentencing habits, then the inability to talk in chambers made no difference in the disposition process. But if the attorney did not know the particular judge, then the case would probably be transferred to short cause, where the judges almost always chamberized with attorneys about sentencing.

When an S.O.T. trial substituted for a guilty plea, the defense attorney would often simply say, "We submit," or, "Submitted," without any argument in court. Or, the attorney would argue for several minutes on behalf of his client even though he knew that the case would result in conviction. In this situation, the S.O.T. hearing was used to enter background or mitigating information designed to influence the judge in sentencing. The attorney's argument might also be designed to impress his client. Or, it might be to preserve a record of the case in the event of later appeal. In these "dead bang" cases, the S.O.T. hearing functioned as a "slow plea," as described by Levin (1972, 1977) on the Pittsburgh courts and by White (1971) and Alschuler (1968) on the Philadelphia courts.

Note that the prosecutor's role in these "dead bang" marijuana cases was a passive one. He did not care about sentencing and was content to let the judge reduce the case to a misdemeanor. The D.A. office policy specifically restricted reduction of drug charges, but allowed dismissal of other charges (in conjunction with a conviction on the marijuana charge). Thus, individual D.A.s were limited in their discretion, and most defense attorneys knew this. In the following marijuana case, the defense attorney (private) was not familiar with the norms of the court. When the case was called, the attorney announced, "Ready for jury trial." The D.A. went over to talk to the attorney and they whispered for about a minute; then the attorney and his client went outside. A few minutes later, both attorneys were chamberizing with the judge regarding the likely sentence on a change of plea. In chambers, the judge heard a brief description of the case and said, "As a matter of course, I'd make it a misdemeanor by Penal Code Section 17, and impose a small fine." The defense attorney seemed to think, and acted with his client, as if he had been able to arrange the misdemeanor disposition *because* of his "threat" of jury trial. But, in fact, the case was a typical one (young defendant with no record, employed, small quantity of marijuana) and the final disposition was quite standard (guilty plea to felony with misdemeanor sentence). This disposition depended upon the *judge's* agreement to a misdemeanor sentence; the prosecutor had conceded nothing—he simply suggested to the defense attorney that he chamberize with the judge.

The restrictive D.A. office policies on charge reduction and dismissal actually placed the prosecutors in a strong bargaining position. Schelling (1963:22) pointed out that

> the power to constrain an adversary may depend on the power to bind oneself; that, in bargaining, weakness if often strength, freedom may be freedom to capitulate. . . .

Thus, while the defense was free to negotiate or go to trial, that freedom must be viewed in the context of alternatives determined by prosecutors and judges. A distinctive feature of a bargaining situation is that

> the ability of one participant to gain his ends is dependent to an important degree on the choices or decisions that the other participant will make (Schelling, 1963:5).

To the extent that the defense wished to minimize the sentence and conviction level, it was dependent upon decisions of the prosecution and judge.

I have characterized the bargaining involved in most "light, dead bang" cases as *implicit*. No promises were made and the precise nature of the bargain was not usually spelled out. Instead, the bargain was understood or implied by the nature of the disposition, with predictably lenient treatment for cases settled without trial. There was often communication regarding the outcome of the case, as seen in chamberizing with judges over the sentence. Or, a disposition would be arranged without direct communication, but with a tacit awareness of the consequences of a certain guilty plea or slow plea before a particular judge. One judge (who was on committees actively studying the court processes) distinguished between preplea discussions which were "actual plea bargains" and those which were not. This distinction is similar to that described here between explicit and implicit bargains. The judge said,

> There is a large universe of practices which, for lack of a better word, I shall call "preplea discussions" regarding the outcome of a case. A subset of these practices are the "actual plea bargains." But preplea discussions encompass a much larger range than plea bargaining, and is actually a more appropriate way of talking about what goes on in court these days.

When I asked the judge to describe some preplea discussions which were not actual plea bargains, he continued,

> On a three-count forgery case, the defense attorney asks the D.A., "Can I have one count?" The D.A. says, "Yes, which one?" The defense attorney says, "Count 2." And that's it. No bargain has been made. No promise made that counts 1 and 3 will be dismissed in exchange for the plea to count 2. *It's simply that everyone knows what the standard practice is.* Or here's another example. The defense attorney comes into court and asks the D.A., "What does Judge Hall give on bookmaking cases?" The D.A. asks if there are any priors. The attorney says, "No," and the D.A. says, "He usually gives $150 fine on the first offense." The attorney says, "Fine. We'll enter a plea to count one." Again no promise was made by anybody. *It's just that everyone knows what customarily will happen.* This is what I mean by the larger arena of preplea discussions [emphasis added].

I use the general term "implicit plea bargaining" to describe several different kinds of dispositions which I observed in Los Angeles. On the one hand, there was the "standard practice," described by the judge above, of dismissing all remaining counts when there was a guilty plea (or slow plea) to one count. A similar standard practice was the prosecutorial reduction of charges on those offenses which were routinely charged at a higher level than the expected conviction. These were the cases in which charge reduction was almost automatic, as long as there were no aggravating conditions in the case. Plea bargains such as these perhaps used to involve explicit negotiation but had since become institutionalized.

Another type of implicit plea bargain was the plea of guilty (or slow plea) as charged in anticipation of sentence leniency. With "light" cases in Los Angeles one might ask whether such a disposition was a bargain at all, since sentences in these cases were generally not affected by the method of case disposition. For example, a defendant in a "light, dead bang" case would have almost nothing to lose by a full trial, and he might gain a complete acquittal (since there was always a chance of acquittal in any adversary trial). But in this situation defendants often valued the certainty of a lenient sentence over the possible but highly unlikely chance of acquittal. The benefit of certainty and the wish to get the case over with cannot be quantified like that of a sentence differential, but they can still be of significant value to defendants facing criminal charges. In addition, the defense attorney could pursue his own interests by recommending nontrial disposition in a "light, dead bang" case. He minimized his time per case and he saved his time and energy in trial for those cases in which he felt the client had the most to gain by full-fledged trial. Thus, while the disposition process in the "light, dead bang" case involved elements of implicit negotiation, the process could also be described in terms of the shared values and norms of the court participants.

"Reasonable Doubt" Cases

While most marijuana possession cases presented strong evidence for conviction, there were two main arguments used by defense to seek dismissal or acquittal. The first argument rested on questions of admissibility of the evidence, and the second depended upon the weakness of the evidence itself. Where evidence was obtained by illegal means (for example, police lacked probable cause to search, or the search otherwise violated the defendant's constitutional rights), then it was not admissible in court, by virtue of the exclusionary rule. Defense motions to suppress evidence were made in a separate hearing before trial. This evidentiary hearing (called a "1538.5 motion") was usually scheduled several weeks before the trial date. If the defense motion was granted and the evidence suppressed, then the case would be dismissed. But if the defense motion was denied, then the case would be handled like any other "dead bang" marijuana case, that is, with a guilty plea or a slow plea. Immediately after denial of the motion, the attorneys would talk briefly (and perhaps chamberize with the judge) to dispose of the case right then, rather than waiting until the trial date.

In the following case, the defense attorney argued a "1538.5 motion" to suppress the evidence (marijuana). The legality of the search rested on the credibility of the defendant against that of the two arresting officers. During this evidentiary hearing, the officers testified that they saw the defendant emerge from his house at about 11:30 P.M. and begin walking down the street. The police, who were sitting in their patrol car, then saw the defendant throw "what appeared to be a small, shiny metal object" from his pocket onto the sidewalk. The police left their car, stopped the defendant, and retrieved the metal object from the ground. The object was a snuffbox containing marijuana, and the police arrested the defendant for possession. After the two policemen described their version of what happened, the defendant took the stand. The defendant was white, in his early twenties, and well-dressed, but with very long hair. He had no prior criminal record and was represented by a private attorney. In a calm, articulate manner, the defendant recounted an entirely different version of what had happened.

According to the defendant, as he left his house to go to a nearby coffee shop, a police car slowly followed him down the street. The police then shone a spotlight on him, got out of their car, and told him they were looking for a man with weapons (because of recent trouble in the area). The defendant was asked what was in his pocket and he showed them keys and a wallet from the outside pockets of his coat. The police then searched the inside pockets of his coat, without asking or obtaining the defendant's permission to do so, and found the snuffbox of marijuana. They then placed the defendant under arrest for possession. On cross-examination, the defendant denied making any "throwing" motion before the police stopped him. He also admitted, on the stand, that the snuffbox *was* in his pocket and that he knew that it contained marijuana.

This kind of case was called a "throwing" case; the circumstances of the arrest were very common for drug cases of all kinds.[2] Defense attorneys were especially annoyed by "throwing" cases because the police version of the arrest was always the same and was invariably accepted by the judge. There were rarely any other witnesses, so the issue was one of the defendant's word against the policeman's. Indeed, at the conclusion of the pretrial hearing in this case, the judge announced:

> The issue here is simply one of credibility. If the defendant is telling the truth, then it was an out-and-out roust by the police. I cannot accept that. I must believe the word of the arresting officers. Motion denied.

The defense attorney whispered to the D.A. for about a minute, and then stated to the court that there would be a change of plea. The D.A. began to take the waivers for a guilty plea when the defendant balked, saying, "No, I am *not* pleading guilty voluntarily. I want a jury trial." The defense attorney (who had not conferred with his client after the motion was denied) was very embarrassed and whispered furiously at the defendant. The attorney apologized to the judge for the "boy's behavior," adding in a paternal way: "I've known this boy since he was born, Your Honor. I know his family very well. He's just a little confused."

The judge interrupted the attorney to ask the defendant directly whether he wanted to plead guilty. The defendant said bitterly (over the frantic whispers of his counsel), "No, I think this is entirely unfair. I'm being railroaded." Whereupon, the judge refused to accept the guilty plea and there was a short recess.

It was not uncommon to see a defendant "confused" in this way by the disposition arranged by his attorney. Most defense attorneys tried to explain the proceedings to their clients beforehand, but even with an explanation, defendants were often bewildered. When a defendant completely balked at a plea bargain, as in this case, there was usually a short recess to give the attorney a chance to confer with his client. The defendant invariably returned to court ready to accept the nontrial disposition. In this case, the attorney told his client that there was absolutely *no* chance of acquittal at trial: the motion to suppress evidence was the key issue; they had lost that motion and the defendant had admitted, in sworn testimony, that he had possessed the marijuana; therefore, they had no case for trial. Finally, the defendant reluctantly agreed to waive his right to jury trial and change his plea to guilty. The disposition took place in court several minutes later.

In marijuana cases where the evidence itself was weak, there was usually a chance of complete acquittal.[3] To seek an acquittal, defense attorneys might discuss the case with the D.A., hoping to arrange a dismissal or an S.O.T. trial for not guilty. Defense attorneys chose this option only if the D.A. was perceived to be amenable and the prosecution's case was weak. The D.A.s needed permission from their superiors to formally dismiss a case. However, D.A.s could evade this requirement by informally arranging with the judge to dismiss by an S.O.T. trial for not guilty. For example, a P.D. described one D.A. who was not intimidated by office pressures against dismissing cases:

> In Beal's court, the D.A. was good. He'd come into chambers and tell the judge, "Look, I've got this case, and I think the cop is lying, so I don't want to call him as a witness." And Judge Beal would dismiss the case.

Another D.A. described how he used the S.O.T. proceeding for a not-guilty verdict, and he explained his considerations in agreeing to such a disposition:

> If you've got an exceptional case—*one which is weak and there's a good chance that the defendant may be innocent*—then you don't want to take it before a jury because you never know what they'll do. And besides you don't want to try it because it's such a bad case. So you chamberize with the judge and agree to S.O.T. with a not-guilty verdict.... For example, where there is direct evidence for the corpus of a crime but only indirect evidence to link the defendant to the crime. That is, there could be a completely innocent explanation of the defendant's connection to the scene. If it's a weak case but I'm

convinced he's guilty, then I'll try it. But *on a weak case where the
defendant could be innocent, I don't like to trust the vagaries of a jury*
[emphasis added].

In one case I observed, there was a question as to whether the quantity of
marijuana found on the defendant was sufficient to sustain a conviction. The
attorneys chamberized with the judge and then the defendant submitted the case
to the court on the basis of the transcript of the preliminary hearing. In court,
the D.A. said simply, "We submit." Then the defense attorney (a P.D.) argued
that the total substance of marijuana found was .9 gram, of which 60 percent
was seeds and stems, and further, that even the narcotics expert for the
prosecution had been unable to identify how much narcotic substance was
present, according to the testimony in the transcript. The D.A. offered a weak,
general comment in response, and the judge found the defendant not guilty on
the basis of insufficient quantity.

In another instance, the P.D. had taken a marijuana case to jury trial and the
jury hung 10-2 for acquittal. The case was then assigned to a different
courtroom for a retrial. In the new court, the attorneys spoke briefly to the
judge in chambers and, a few minutes later, the case was submitted to the court
on the transcript. There was no argument from either side, and the judge found
the defendant not guilty.

This use of a brief, informal trial (the S.O.T. proceeding) as a slow plea of
not guilty appears to be unique to Los Angeles. There are frequent references in
the literature to the use of shortened trials as slow pleas of *guilty* (Alschuler
1968; Levin 1972, 1977; White 1971). But, other than in studies of Los Angeles
Superior Court, there is no mention of the trial operating as an informal
mechanism for negotiated acquittal.[4]

In deciding whether to seek acquittal by full trial or by negotiated
disposition, a defense attorney considered the obvious weaknesses of the
evidence and his perception of the D.A.'s willingness to agree to an acquittal. In
addition, the defense attorney considered the judge's willingness to acquit, and
the amount of time that the attorney felt he could spend on the case in full trial.
For example, in one very weak marijuana case, the P.D. decided upon a full jury
trial. The D.A. agreed that the case was a weak one and he regretted that he did
not have the authority to dismiss it. During the trial, after the prosecution had
concluded its case, the defense attorney asked for a directed verdict of acquittal.
The judge granted the motion and dismissed the case. The P.D. explained to me
why he had chosen jury trial rather than S.O.T. for not guilty: "Whenever
there's any doubt on what the judge might do, I don't take any chances. *I'll try
it before a jury as long as I've got the time* [emphasis added]."

I asked the P.D. if the judge would have indicated beforehand (in chambers)
if he would agree to acquittal by S.O.T. The P.D. said, "Yes. . . . This judge is
great. *But I don't like to press him.* This way he could have let the jury do it
[emphasis added]."

Having decided against any type of negotiated acquittal, a defense attorney usually recommended jury, rather than court, trial for marijuana cases because the cases so often depended upon police testimony. Defense attorneys believed that juries were more likely than judges "to call the cops liars," in the words of one P.D. The next two marijuana cases illustrate the resolution of "reasonable doubt" cases by jury trial. In each case, the defense attorney chose not to discuss the matter with the D.A. before trial. Both cases were "throwing" cases (described earlier), but they were not typical, since the defendants each had witnesses to corroborate their testimony.

During the trial of the first case, the two arresting officers described the case as follows:

> The officers were patrolling Griffith Park. At 10:30 P.M. they came upon a group of about ten youths standing by their cars talking. The officers saw one youth [whom they identified as the defendant] throw what appeared to be two cigarettes into the bushes. They retrieved the cigarettes, decided that they contained marijuana, and arrested the defendant for possession.

After the prosecution presented its case, the defendant took the stand and denied that he had held the cigarettes or that he had made any "throwing" motion. Then, in the true style of Perry Mason surprises, one of the other youths from the park took the stand and confessed that *he,* not the defendant, had possessed the marijuana, and that *he* had thrown the cigarettes into the bushes when the police arrived. Needless to say, that testimony raised considerable doubt in the minds of the jurors as to the credibility of the officers, and the jury returned a verdict of not guilty. After the trial, I asked the defense attorney (a P.D.) why the defendant's friend admitted his possession, and what would happen now in terms of further prosecution. The P.D. said,

> There was a lot of peer group pressure on him to testify. He won't get too much trouble for it because he's a juvenile. He'll be charged now through the juvenile division.

The bailiff in court was angry that his two colleagues (Los Angeles County Sheriffs) had lied so blatantly on the stand. The bailiff said,

> Do you know what that sergeant said to me after the trial? "We don't bother to arrest juveniles. You just waste a lot of time filling out forms and nothing ever happens to them anyway." Biff [the defendant] was the *only* adult in the group of ten kids. *That's* why they arrested him, not because they ever saw him with the stuff!

In the second case, two police officers testified that they observed the defendant walking down the street one afternoon. When the defendant spotted the patrol car in the distance, according to police, he threw a small plastic bag onto the sidewalk. The officers then stopped the defendant, identified marijuana in the bag, and arrested him for possession. In the defense presentation (at jury trial), the defendant testified that he did not have any marijuana and had made no "throwing" motion. In addition, a friend of the defendant who had been walking down the street from the other direction corroborated the defendant's testimony. In this situation, there was again a clear issue of credibility of the two arresting officers, the defendant, and his friend. However, there was no ready explanation for the presence of a bag of marijuana on the sidewalk.

Although the P.D. in this case decided that there was a chance of acquittal before a jury, other defense attorneys might not have been so optimistic. A different defense attorney might have evaluated this case as "dead bang" and argued the credibility issue in a pretrial motion for suppression of evidence (as in a similar case described earlier). Such a motion might have impressed the client and certainly would have taken less time than a full trial, although it probably would have been denied. I asked the P.D. who handled the case why it went to jury trial and he answered,

> He [the defendant] claimed he was innocent. But also, . . . ever since . . . [the D.A.'s] campaign started, the policy from the office is "No deals on narcotics cases." Before, with a marijuana case we could plead to the straight misdemeanor of 11556—"Being in a place where marijuana is used." Now we can't plead to anything.

The fact that the defendant had a witness to testify on his behalf bolstered his "claim" to innocence, but it appeared that the P.D. was not entirely convinced by the defendant's story. The P.D. was annoyed at the change of prosecutorial policy on reductions in narcotics cases. So, to an extent, his decision to go for jury trial in this case seemed to be influenced by his desire to retaliate against the D.A.'s office.[5]

This particular P.D. was also a very talented trial advocate, and he raised several persuasive arguments in presentation to the jury. For example, the P.D. noted that no fingerprints had been introduced from the bag of marijuana. The P.D. commented later that it was police policy *never* to fingerprint plastic bags because of the difficulty of obtaining any usable prints from plastic. But the inexperienced D.A., ignorant of that police policy, could not respond to the P.D.'s argument. At the conclusion of the trial, the defendant was acquitted.

Possession of Dangerous Drugs

"Pill cases," as they were commonly called, usually involved violation of Section 11910, Health and Safety Code, an optional felony offense making it illegal to possess dangerous drugs. The drugs involved were usually "uppers" or "downers"; opiates were covered by a different offense category. The typical pill case was similar to the typical marijuana case—a young defendant, small quantity of contraband, and factual and legal issues surrounding the arrest similar to those in a marijuana case. As with marijuana cases, the D.A.s would not reduce 11910 charges, but judges generally imposed misdemeanor sentences. The disposition process for pill cases was essentially the same as that described above for marijuana cases. Three cases involving possession of dangerous drugs are discussed below to illustrate the disposition of this offense. The first one was a "dead bang" case; the second was an "overfiled reasonable doubt" case; and the last one was "reasonable doubt" with a chance of acquittal.

The first pill case was transferred to short cause from its scheduled trial department by agreement between the P.D. and D.A. The defendant was in custody, so his attorney pressed for immediate sentencing. The P.D. and D.A. went into the judge's chambers (in short cause) during a recess, and the judge opened the discussion as follows:

Judge: What have you got today, boys?

P.D.: The Murray Enton case, sir. It's a straight submission of possession of dangerous drugs. He had fourteen pills on him. It's his first offense. We'd like it made a misdemeanor, and we'd like immediate sentencing.

Judge [to D.A.]: What do you have on his record?

D.A.: No record on him.

P.D.: Immediate sentencing, then?

Judge: Sure, since he doesn't have a record.

P.D.: He's been in custody about 110 days.

Judge: I'll give him ninety days with credit for time served. Released forthwith.

P.D.: Thank you, Your Honor.

In court there were several minutes of argument accompanying the submission. The P.D. pointed out that the defendant was unconscious at the time the contraband was found on him. The D.A. responded with the observation that the defendant was probably unconscious because he was under the influence of the pills, and besides, that was not a defense against the charge of possession. The judge found the defendant guilty and sentenced him according to the conversation in chambers. Although there was brief argument during this S.O.T. proceeding, the submission operated as a slow plea of guilty. Included in the formal "waivers" taken by the D.A. was the defendant's stipulation that "in all probability" he would be found guilty. This stipulation was required by the California Supreme Court decision *In re Mosley* (83 Cal. Rptr. 809, 1970) in situations such as this where submission on the transcript was the functional equivalent of a guilty plea. A slow plea of guilty was sometimes called a *"Mosley S.O.T."*

The second case contained two drug charges: count 1 was a violation of Section 11911 (Health and Safety Code)—possession of dangerous drugs for purpose of sale (a mandatory felony), and count 2 was a violation of Section 11910—possession of dangerous drugs (also called "straight possession"). Count 1 was considered an "overfiled" count and the attorneys negotiated explicitly to reduce the charge to one of straight possession. Because of restrictions on the D.A.'s authority to reduce charges, the attorneys used the S.O.T. proceeding, with cooperation of the judge, to reach a conviction on the lesser charge. The P.D. and D.A. went into the judge's chambers and described the case to him:

P.D.:   There are two counts here. Count 1 is 11911—that's for the 500 reds, the "downers." And count 2 is 11910, 'cause he also had a few "uppers."

Judge   [looking over the case file]: Hmmm, this was sent over here from Juvenile?

P.D.:   Yes. He's just eighteen. But because of large quantity, they wouldn't touch it over in Juvenile. We'd like to submit it on count 1 for a straight possession and let the court do whatever it wants on sentencing when the probation report comes back. I should tell you, too, Judge, that the boy is on juvenile probation for a burglary.

          [Judge looks over to the D.A. for his comment.]

D.A.:   Yes. We'll submit it on 11910 as a necessary lesser included offense of count 1—the 11911 on the reds. And a guilty finding on that.

Judge: What do you want to do about the other count?

D.A.:   Put it over to the P and S [probation and sentencing hearing].

The disposition worked out on this case was fairly common, although it appears complicated. Why, one might ask, did not the D.A. simply agree to acquittal on count 1 and conviction on count 2? The reason is that the prosecutors preferred to have the conviction on the count which most accurately described the defendant's involvement in the offense. This meant a stronger hold on the defendant upon any violation of probation, or as a "prior" conviction for any subsequent offense. In this case, then, the defendant's conviction was for the possession of the 500 "downers," not the few "uppers."

The last question and response in the chambers conversation above also reflected a standard procedure. Whenever additional counts were to be dismissed, they were not dismissed at the time of the disposition. Instead they were "put over to the P and S," which meant that they would be dismissed at the sentencing hearing after the probation report had been finished. Thus, in the event that any serious information damaging to the defendant was uncovered by the probation officer, the court and prosecutor would still have an additional claim on the defendant. This, of course, provided an incentive for the defense attorney to represent his client's background as accurately as possible in the plea negotiations.

Before the D.A. took the waivers from the defendant in this case, the judge formally explained to him the nature of the explicit plea bargain:

> A conference was held in chambers. I'm aware of your background. I know that Juvenile sent you over here, and that you're on juvenile court probation for burglary. Mr. Arney [the D.A.], Mr. Hier [the P.D.], and I have agreed that my reading of this transcript will be for the lesser included offense of count 1, which is 11910, an optional felony. I have no preconceived ideas on sentencing at this point. I will decide the sentence after I see your probation report. Now, do you fully understand the nature of the plea bargain?

The defendant nodded in agreement. At the probation and sentencing hearing four weeks later, count 2 was dismissed "in the interests of justice." The defendant was placed on probation for three years with the first thirty days to be spent in county jail.

"Reasonable doubt" pill cases had the same sorts of issues as "reasonable doubt" marijuana cases. If there was a question of admissibility of evidence, it was usually raised by a pretrial motion. But if the evidence itself was weak, then most defense attorneys sought an acquittal, either through trial or a negotiated disposition. The following pill case presents an interesting variation on a negotiated disposition for acquittal. In this case, there were three defendants (Durgin, Payne, and Lord), each charged with two counts—one count of 11910 (pills), and one count of P.C. Sec. 12025, a misdemeanor, which makes it illegal to carry a concealed weapon. All three defendants were represented by the same private attorney, but there were different issues pertaining to each defendant. The D.A. and defense attorney described the case to the trial judge in chambers before submitting it on the transcript. The D.A. began:

> *D.A.:*   These three guys are driving along and something's funny. . . . What was it? [turns to defense attorney]
>
> *Def. Atty.:* The police noticed that the car was weaving all over the road, so they pulled them over.
>
> *D.A.*   [continuing the story]: Yeah, so then they see this guy in the back seat. He's a moron and he's stuffing pills all over. They're falling out of his pockets and everything. Then the police see a pistol in the back seat. It's not concealed at all. As the police go into the car, they see Durgin—he's the moron—stuffing a Darvon box into his pocket. In the box

are "bennies" and Payne's name is on the box. Payne then goes into a stupor—presumably from the drugs. OK. There's no question about Lord. He's guilty. And the Durgin case should be kicked out—not guilty.

Def. Atty.: We agree on that, but we disagree on the Payne case. No drugs were found on his person. I think he should be found not guilty.

D.A.: I think he's guilty. We'll let you decide [on the basis of the transcript].

Judge: OK, I'll read it. Hold Lord on one count pills; kick Durgin out; and decide on Payne, right?

D.A.: Right.

Judge: Now on any of them, I'll need a probation report.

Def. Atty.: OK, there's not much record on them. Few drunks, that's all.

There are several interesting points in this case. First, the D.A. readily agreed that the misdemeanor weapons count did *not* hold up against any of the defendants, since there was no evidence to show that the pistol was concealed. Second, the attorneys agreed that the defendant Lord, who was driving the car, should be convicted of possession of the pills. And they agreed that "the moron Durgin" should be acquitted. Presumably this agreement was based on the fact that his subnormal mental capacity made him incapable of commiting a crime, since the evidence clearly showed that he had possessed the pills. Yet there was no evidence entered, either in chambers or in the S.O.T. session in court, on Durgin's mental state or criminal capacity. The D.A. simply conceded that this defendant was a moron and therefore should be acquitted. Third, the attorneys disagreed about the strength of the evidence against Payne. The defense attorney argued that there was "reasonable doubt" in Payne's case, but the attorney did not really pursue it. Another attorney, who perhaps had represented *only* that one defendant, might have pushed harder for an acquittal.

Finally, it is interesting how the attorneys defined and narrowed the issues beforehand to present to the judge in chambers. Thus, the judge's reading of the transcript was focused on the *one* point in dispute: whether or not Payne was guilty of possession. In court, the attorneys argued briefly in the S.O.T., calling the judge's attention to the same issues they had discussed in chambers. Then the judge found Lord and Payne guilty on the pills count, Durgin not guilty, and all three defendants were acquitted on the weapons count.

Bookmaking and Homosexuality

Even more than the drug offenses above, the victimless crimes of bookmaking and homosexuality ("sex perversions") were seen by attorneys and judges as unimportant, minor offenses. These cases were a nuisance for the court and were dealt with rapidly. Most participants agreed that the crimes, in their typical form, were deserving of misdemeanor, not felony, treatment; and of course some argued that the "offenses" should not be crimes at all. The "dead bang" cases were settled by guilty plea or slow plea; the sentence was usually a fine or probation without jail. The "reasonable doubt" cases were often resolved by dismissal or S.O.T. for not guilty.

Bookmaking cases were handled quickly and routinely. One D.A. commented that "bookmaking is the lowest offense. We only use a short form plea there because no one is going to appeal that." By using a "short form plea," the D.A. meant that he did not go through the entire set of questions on the defendant's waiver of his constitutional rights. One morning in short cause, I observed three different bookmaking cases in sequence, examples of routine case processing. There was no discussion in chambers beforehand, and the entire proceeding in court for all three cases took less than ten minutes. In each case the defendant changed his plea of not guilty to guilty of count 1 of bookmaking and counts 2 and 3 (if there were any) were dismissed. The probation reports were waived, and the defendants were fined from $100 to $200 (the differences in the fines were said to be due to the differences in the defendants' prior records).

Acts of homosexuality were prosecuted under P.C. Sec. 288a, an optional felony which prohibited "sex perversions," specifically oral copulation. The normal crime of Sec. 288a involved consenting adults with little or no criminal record. Most cases were settled by nontrial disposition with misdemeanor sentence; conviction was either on the optional felony as charged or on the lesser offense of disorderly conduct, P.C. Sec. 647, a misdemeanor.[6] Because of the D.A. office policy restricting charge reduction, the S.O.T. proceeding was sometimes used to allow the judge to convict on the lesser charge. For example, in the following case of homosexual conduct, the D.A. and two private attorneys agreed upon the charge reduction and then went into chambers to confirm it with the judge:

Def. Atty.: What we have here is a garden variety 288a. No priors on either one. We'd like to make it 647(b), a misdemeanor.

D.A.: I've talked to Adams [D.A. head of trials] and he's OK'd it to amend the information to indicate the 647(b).

Def. Atty.: My client is a graduate student in sociology working for the county. They won't give him any trouble, we hope. We'd like immediate sentencing—we'll waive the probation report.

Judge: Any time?

Def. Atty.: No.

Judge: OK, I'll fine them.

The judge's last question was relevant to his sentencing decision: had the defendants served time in custody pending their disposition, the judge would have sentenced them to whatever time they had already served. "Time served" was often an alternative sentence to a fine, especially in "light" cases. In court, the case was settled by an S.O.T. with *Mosley* waivers, with no argument or discussion by attorneys. Defendants were convicted of the lesser charge of Sec. 647(b); they waived the probation report and were each fined $250.

Forgery and Bad Checks

Forgery and bad checks cases were most commonly "light, dead bang" cases. Because of the nature of the physical evidence, the cases were usually quite strong for the prosecution. Typically the defendants had minimal criminal records and not a great deal of money was involved. Cases generally included several counts of the same charge, since each forged or bad check passed comprised a new and separate offense. These cases were generally settled by a nontrial conviction on one count with dismissal of remaining counts. The D.A.'s dismissal of the extra counts was virtually automatic with a guilty plea or S.O.T. disposition. Forgery and bad checks were optional felonies; the conviction was usually for the felony as charged but then it was often made a misdemeanor by sentence. Probation was a common sentence for these offenses, usually with the condition that the defendant make restitution to the victim. Bargaining to reach this outcome was implicit, unless the defendant's record or circumstances of the offense presented aggravating conditions.

In one forgery case the two codefendants were each charged with six counts of forgery, involving a total of $850 in forged checks. The defendants had been in custody almost four months awaiting their trial date. The defense attorneys (a P.D. and a court-appointed private attorney) arranged with the prosecutor the morning of trial to transfer the case to a short cause court. A primary interest of the defense was to obtain immediate sentencing (without a probation report) since preparation of the report would mean an additional three to four weeks of custody for the defendants. In short cause the defendants pled guilty to count 1 of forgery and the D.A. dismissed the remaining five counts. The judge agreed to immediate sentencing and gave the defendants probation and a six-month suspended jail sentence—suspended on the condition that restitution be made to the victim. The defendants were then released from custody.

In a second case, the defendant was charged with two counts of bad checks[7] with a prior conviction of bad checks. The defendant was O.R. (own recognizance release), and represented by a private attorney. The attorneys agreed on a misdemeanor disposition and chamberized with the judge in short cause to arrange it. There was a heavy caseload in court that morning and there were about six other attorneys in chambers at that same time, so the discussion on this case was brief:

D.A.:   This is an N.S.F. [not sufficient funds] charge with a prior N.S.F. We're talking about a misdemeanor here.

Judge: Is he going to plead to the misdemeanor?

D.A.:   No, I can't do that [referring to his lack of authority to reduce the *charge* to a misdemeanor].

Judge: You've got a deal. I'll go by Section 17 to the misdemeanor [referring to the common practice of making the conviction a misdemeanor by *sentence*].

In court, the defendant pled guilty as charged to count 1 (an optional felony) and count 2 was put over to the probation and sentencing hearing. No indication was made, for the record, of the judge's promise in chambers to make the offense a misdemeanor by P.C. Sec. 17. This oversight was not unusual, since most nontrial dispositions were worked out in the context of mutual trust and a common understanding of normal patterns of sentencing.

Auto Theft

The offense of grand theft auto, an optional felony, was usually charged along with the lesser offense of felony joy riding (driving without consent) and/or receiving stolen property. These two lesser offenses were also optional felonies, but they carried a lighter maximum punishment than grand theft auto [hereafter in this section, G.T.A.]. Defense attorneys considered most G.T.A. cases to be "overfiled." Typically there was a chance of acquittal on the G.T.A. charge but a good chance of conviction on one of the lesser charges. As one P.D. said,

> Most G.T.A.s are really joy riding anyway. It's so hard to prove grand theft auto. The way it's done it's like Russian roulette: a kid drives a hot car for a few days and then he gives it to a friend. The friend drives it just a bit and then gives it to someone else and on and on. All the time they know it's stolen and that someone will get caught.

Most G.T.A. cases were settled by a guilty plea or S.O.T. conviction of the lesser felony offense of joy riding or receiving stolen property. Unless the defendant had a bad prior record, this lesser felony charge was then typically made a misdemeanor by sentence.

In one auto theft case, a twenty-year-old Mexican-American woman was charged with G.T.A., felony joy riding, and burglary. She was represented by a P.D. and her case went directly to short cause from the arraignment in Dept. A, in anticipation of a nontrial disposition. Before court convened, her attorney went into the judge's chambers with the D.A. The attorneys emerged from chambers and the P.D. went over to the defendant and said, "He [the D.A.] will take a joy riding and dismiss the burglary and the G.T.A." The young woman was obviously relieved and beamed at this news. Then the P.D. explained all the questions which would be asked of her in court. At one point, the defendant became angry and said, "Wait a minute. I thought you said that joy riding was a misdemeanor!" The P.D. answered,

> At the time of sentencing, the judge will make it a misdemeanor. If the judge sentences you to probation or to the youth authority, then it's a misdemeanor. That's what will probably happen. Although I can't promise you that.

An interesting aspect of this case is the fact that the attorneys had *not* been talking to the judge in chambers and the judge had *not* indicated that he would make the offense a misdemeanor. The judge was ill that morning and had not come to court; the attorneys were simply using his chambers for their discussion. And the attorneys were both assuming the normal outcome for a G.T.A. case on a defendant with little or no record—namely, that after a plea to joy riding, the offense is made a misdemeanor by sentence. After the P.D.'s discussion with his client, the clerk announced that the judge would not be in court but that another judge would be over shortly to handle the morning's cases. When the other judge came, the defendant pled guilty to joy riding and the case was continued three weeks for the presentence investigation. At the sentence hearing, a completely new judge was sitting in the court. The record was unavailable to check the conclusion of this case, but it would have been very unusual for the new judge to deviate from the standard sentencing pattern, in view of the implicit plea bargain.

In another auto theft case, the evidence was very weak for the prosecution and the defense decided there was a good chance of complete acquittal. The defendant, represented by a P.D., was charged with G.T.A. and receiving stolen property, and the case went to jury trial. During an early recess in the trial, the D.A. discussed the case with me:

D.A.: This is a bad case. We can't really tie the two counts together. The defendant had a garage in which a stripped, stolen car was found, and he says he rented the garage out. On the theft charge, it's really weak because he was never seen in the car. And on the receiving stolen property, we have no proof that he had any *knowledge* that the car was stolen. But what can you do? We gotta put it on, and we just might convince a jury.

L.M.M.: Isn't there something else you could have done?

D.A.: We couldn't dispose of it. We would have taken a plea to anything, but the guy said he was innocent. But, hell, if he was innocent, why wouldn't he give the name and address of the person he was renting to? And show rent receipts on the garage?

L.M.M.: Maybe because the guy is a friend of his?

D.A.:   Exactly. Or else it's all just a story. He's guilty at some level
for sure! There are whole gangs of car strippers—they steal the
car, sell the parts, and junk it.

In the defense presentation, the defendant testified that the person to
whom he had rented the garage did not pay the rent regularly and that the
defendant tried to evict him. In fact, the defendant had contacted a lawyer for
advice on eviction and the lawyer came to the trial and corroborated the
defendant's explanation. There were several other contradictory points brought
out for both sides, and other witnesses were called to testify. The trial lasted
three days and ended with a hung jury, 11-1 for not guilty. After the trial, the
judge told the D.A. privately that he thought the verdict was a "miscarriage of
justice" and that the defendant should have been convicted. The D.A. handling
the case wanted to dismiss the charges, but because of the judge's view, his
superior (the calendar deputy D.A. for the courtroom) recommended scheduling
the case for retrial. I could not follow this case to its conclusion, but the charges
were probably dismissed in an S.O.T. for not guilty once the case reached its
new courtoom.

Burglary

Burglary consisted of the entry of a building or vehicle with the specific intent
to commit grand or petit larceny, or any felony. Most burglary cases were
charged in the second degree, an optional felony. First-degree burglary, a
mandatory felony, was any burglary committed while armed with a deadly
weapon, or any burglary committed at night. Cases of first-degree burglary are
discussed in the next chapter, while typical second-degree burglaries (which were
"light" cases) are discussed here.

In a "dead bang" burglary, the defense would point out any mitigating
factors in the defendant's background or in the offense to arrange a nontrial
disposition with a misdemeanor sentence. The D.A.s preferred a guilty plea or
slow plea to the felony charge of burglary with the understanding that the judge
would make it a misdemeanor by sentence. But occasionally the D.A.s would
agree to reduce the burglary to a misdemeanor charge, such as petty theft or
trespass. Actual charge reduction occurred primarily in cases which were weak
for the prosecution.

The following "dead bang" burglary was settled by a guilty plea with
implicit bargaining between the P.D. and D.A. The defendant was a young
Mexican-American, in custody. On the morning of the trial date, the P.D.
arranged with the D.A. to transfer to short cause. The P.D. was familiar with the
judge's sentencing practices in short cause and, since the court was busy that

afternoon, the attorneys did not chamberize with Judge Greene before disposition. In court the defendant pled guilty to burglary and asked for immediate sentencing:

P.D.:   Your Honor, we request immediate sentencing and waive the probation report.

Judge: What's his record?

P.D.:   He has a prior drunk and a G.T.A. [grand theft auto]. Nothing serious. This is really just a shoplifting case. He did enter the K-Mart with the intent to steal. But really all we have here is a petty theft.

Judge: What do the people have?

D.A.:   Nothing either way.

Judge: Any objections to immediate sentencing?

D.A.:   No.

Judge: How long has he been in?

P.D.:   Eighty-three days.

Judge: I make this a misdemeanor by Penal Code Section 17 and sentence you to ninety days in county jail with credit for time served.

Interestingly, the P.D. referred to offenses in terms of their social reality rather than their legal definitions. That is, *legally* the case was a burglary, but *"really"* it was just a petty theft. Likewise, grand theft auto was a serious crime according to the penal code, but because of the circumstances which typically surrounded it, everyone knew it was usually "nothing serious." The P.D. discussed the case afterwards with me and indicated some of his considerations formulating this disposition:

P.D.:   I could have gotten a disposition of a plea to petty theft [a straight misdemeanor]. But, knowing Greene, he'd make it second degree [an optional felony] with a misdemeanor sentence.

L.M.M.:   But why not plead to petty theft, instead of pleading to the felony?

P.D.:   Because petty theft can be counted as a prior.

L.M.M.:   What do you mean?

P.D.:   Petty theft with a prior petty theft or a prior felony conviction is automatically a felony. So with a plea to a felony but with a misdemeanor sentence, that makes this burglary a misdemeanor. Thus, it could not be counted as a prior for petty theft.

Now, if the guy was completely clean and probably never going to get into trouble again, then I'd want him to plead to petty theft, because it looks better on his record. But this kid's in the ghetto and caught up in that and will probably get into trouble again. So it's better for him if he doesn't have a petty theft prior.

Also, you consider the prosecutor. He wants a plea to a felony because it makes their statistics look better. But I know it doesn't really make much difference. Employers or the police go by a guy's rap sheet which shows arrests. And after all, it stays as a felony arrest even if he would have pled to the misdemeanor. But this way, the prosecutor thinks I'm giving him a break. So maybe later he'll give me a break.

A second burglary case was also "dead bang" and resolved by a guilty plea to burglary. The attorneys agreed upon a misdemeanor sentence and chamberized with the judge to arrange the disposition. In this case the defendant was especially concerned about the level of conviction, so his attorney (privately retained) requested that the plea bargain be made part of the court record. Thus, if the judge decided not to make the offense a misdemeanor by sentence (for example, if the probation report came back unfavorable), then the defendant would be allowed to withdraw his plea.

The D.A.'s comments below regarding this plea bargain present an interesting parallel to the P.D.'s comments in the previous burglary case:

D.A.:   In this case I agreed it was worth a misdemeanor disposition, but for me to amend the information adding a misdemeanor count 2, I need the approval of Adams and a lot of bigwigs [D.A. superiors]. . . . I have to fill out a lot of long forms and I couldn't really justify why—for the forms—it should be reduced. *We didn't have a weak case or anything. It's just that the defendant is a good guy.*

L.M.M.:   Did he have any priors?

D.A.:   No felony priors, but a few misdemeanors. In fact, he's on probation now for a petty theft. He's a good character, though—just has an alcoholic problem and he got into this minor trouble when he fell off the wagon.

You see, the defendant didn't want a felony on his record because he wants to enlist in the marines. So the defendant was only interested in the level of sentence. He would have pled to anything to get a misdemeanor.

Of course, the judge and I were simply going on the defense attorney's word that the defendant was a good guy. When the probation report comes in—and it's got complete record checks with the FBI and the state and all—then the judge will know more, and can finally decide on sentencing. *I've done my job for the People. We got a conviction on the felony, and I don't care about the sentence* [emphasis added].

A third burglary case illustrates the actual charge reduction characteristic of "overfiled reasonable doubt" burglary cases. The defendant was charged with burglary of an automobile. The P.D. and D.A. discussed the case and agreed on its crucial weakness: there was no evidence that the car was locked. The attorneys transferred the case to short cause and chamberized with the judge to arrange an S.O.T. trial with conviction on a misdemeanor charge.

> *P.D.:*   We'll submit [S.O.T. trial]. We'd like either an auto tampering or a petty theft. He admits taking the Panasonic, but. . .
>
> *Judge* [interrupting]: Yeah, I've read this transcript. *There's no evidence that the car was locked* [emphasis added].

After the discussion in chambers, the case was submitted on the transcript "with a maximum possible conviction of auto tampering." Because the S.O.T. was a slow plea of guilty, *Mosley* waivers were taken from the defendant: for the record, the defendant acknowledged that "in all probability" he would be found guilty. Indeed, with no additional argument or testimony during the S.O.T., the defendant was found guilty of the misdemeanor of auto tampering.

Assault

Crimes of felonious assault showed tremendous variation in the typical defendants and typical circumstances of the offense, as well as variation in the processes used for disposition. Some assaults were very "serious" cases, either because of aggravated circumstances or a defendant's long record of violent, aggressive behavior. At the other extreme, some assaults were extremely "light"—for example, a family fight, or a barroom fight where the defendant was drunk and had no prior record. In addition, assault cases often had weak cases for the prosecution, simply because of the nature of the offense. Witnesses were sometimes reluctant to testify, or refused to cooperate with the prosecution entirely after the charges had been filed. Also, assault cases were especially likely to involve purely factual disputes—disputes which raised issues of "reasonable doubt" in the minds of judges and jurors.

A "light, dead bang" assault case was usually settled by a guilty plea or slow plea. Depending upon the case, the plea would be to the original charge, to a lesser felony, or to a misdemeanor charge. Generally, the D.A.s would not agree to reduce the charge unless there was weakness in the evidence, but judges often made the original felony conviction a misdemeanor by sentence. Where there were conflicts and weak points in the evidence, the D.A.s were more likely to agree to charge reduction. For example, in one assault case, I overheard the attorneys arguing outside the courtroom about the strength of the evidence. The case was scheduled for trial and witnesses were ready to testify, but the defense attorney (a P.D.) was trying to convince the D.A. to reduce the charge to a misdemeanor battery charge. The D.A. wanted a plea to the felony assault charge (assault with a deadly weapon), and he agreed to let the judge make the case a misdemeanor by sentence. The case involved a landlord/tenant feud where the landlord had threatened the tenant, brandishing a gun, and finally the tenant shot the landlord. In arguing the "equities" of his case, the P.D. attacked the character of the prosecution's key witness, the victim, and built up the strength of the defense position:

> Did you see the elderly black lady sitting in the back of the court? She's their babysitter who was there all night. A very credible witness. She'll testify that the landlord repeatedly threatened my guy with a gun. I mean, this landlord is no angel! He even had turned off the hot water in their apartment. And it was during that bad cold spell in December. They couldn't even wash the baby bottles to feed the baby because of no hot water.

Because of the factual disputes involved in assaults, many "reasonable doubt" cases were resolved by adversary trial or by arranging an S.O.T. for acquittal. For example, in one assault with a deadly weapon case, the prosecution's case rested on the ambiguous testimony of a twelve-year-old girl. The D.A. agreed to chamberize with a judge for acquittal, and they transferred the case to short cause for the disposition. Before the S.O.T. trial, the D.A. said:

> *D.A.:*   May we have a brief conference with Your Honor before we begin?
>
> *Judge*   [smiling]: You mean you want to know what I'm going to do?
>
> *D.A.:*   Counsel does, Your Honor [indicating the P.D.].

After a five-minute conference in chambers, the case was submitted on the transcript and the defendant was found not guilty. This example again shows how the S.O.T. hearing was used as substitute for dismissal.

Conclusion

Regular court participants resolved the "light" cases described in this chapter in a routine, predictable manner. The entire disposition process for these cases rested on the common understanding that (1) the cases were relatively unimportant and offenders would receive lenient sentences, and (2) conflicts over guilt or innocence (which occurred infrequently) could be solved by negotiation or, if necessary, by full trial.

As discussed in chapter 3, judges generally agreed on misdemeanor level sentencing for defendants with little or no record, and for certain offenses. Thus, typical cases involving the offenses described in this chapter had a good chance of probation and no chance of state prison, in spite of the felony designation for these offenses given by the state legislature. Since there was some variation among judges' sentencing decisions, the establishment of short cause courts served to guarantee misdemeanor-level sentencing for "light" cases and to maximize the predictability of the disposition process. The two judges appointed to short cause were generally known to be lenient in sentencing and willing to chamberize with attorneys. Short cause courts thus expedited the disposition process by allowing a quick and easy sorting out of certain cases from the other courtrooms. Unofficial figures from the clerk's office in Los Angeles confirm the importance of short cause: during the last six months of 1970 in the central district, of roughly 6,200 felony dispositions, 1,850 of these dispositions occurred in the two short cause courts. Yet these judges were only two out of twenty-seven in the central district, criminal division; that is, 7 percent of the judges handled 30 percent of the cases.

Prosecutors were mainly interested in obtaining convictions and were generally not concerned with the specifics of sentencing in these "light" cases. Thus, D.A.s agreed to facilitate a disposition with a *misdemeanor sentence* (which depended on judicial discretion) while usually insisting on the guilty plea or slow plea to the the *felony charges*. This particular pattern of disposition with implicit bargaining characterized the "light, dead bang" cases. Where the prosecution's case was weak, D.A.s would engage in bargaining (more likely, explicit) to obtain some conviction, even if on a misdemeanor charge. In very weak cases, D.A.s would either agree to negotiated acquittal (by S.O.T.) or would argue the case in adversary trial.

Where a defense attorney saw real "reasonable doubt" issues in a case, he would either push for dismissal (or acquittal by S.O.T.) or recommend full trial, knowing that his client faced few—if any—sentencing risks from trial in a "light" case. But where the defense attorney saw no chance of acquittal, he would recommend nontrial disposition—guilty plea or slow plea—with the most lenient sentence, given the normal disposition patterns set by judges and prosecutors for different offenses. To an extent the defense attorney was conserving his own time and resources in the handling of the "light, dead bang" case; a trial would probably have entailed few sentencing risks for the defendant and might possibly have led to an acquittal. However, if defense attorneys began taking many "light, dead bang" cases to trial, then the judges might have responded with a sentence penalty for the conviction by trial.

The Dynamics of Case Disposition: The "Serious" Case

While "light" cases were fairly easy to resolve, "serious" cases presented attorneys with more issues of real conflict. Consequently, the disposition process for "serious" cases was difficult and complex. In "light" cases, the D.A.s were not very concerned with sentencing, and the judges tended to impose misdemeanor-level sentences, thus any conflict centered only on the likelihood of conviction. Substantial questions about the strength of the prosecution's case (and the likelihood of conviction) were also involved in "serious" cases. But, in addition, "serious" cases presented very troublesome issues on the severity of the sentence. Reaching agreement on a nontrial disposition in these cases usually involved *explicit* bargaining among the defense attorney, the D.A., and sometimes the judge, while bargaining in "light" cases tended to be *implicit*. Explicit bargaining refers to a process of proposals and counterproposals in which the terms of the final agreement are clearly specified.

Table 5-1 (in chapter 5) indicates how defense attorneys recommended disposition methods based upon the strength and seriousness of a case. In "serious" cases, the recommended disposition was also dependent upon convergence or divergence of D.A. and defense attorney views. The attorneys each evaluated their cases to predict the likelihood of conviction and severity of punishment. Then they compared their expectations and negotiated to resolve differences. Agreement on a nontrial disposition occurred with the convergence of their expectations, while divergence generally led to an adversary trial disposition. Thus, a plea bargain can be described as a point of convergent expectations, based upon Schelling's (1963:114-115) idea that

> the outcome of a bargaining process is to be described most immediately, most straightforwardly, and most empirically in terms of some phenomenon of stabilized convergent expectations. Whether one agrees explicitly to a bargain or agrees tacitly or accepts it by default, he must, if he has his wits about him, expect that he could do no better and recognize that the other party must reciprocate the feeling. Thus the *fact* of an outcome, which is simply a coordinated choice, should be analytically characterized by the notion of converging expectations.

The bargained disposition agreed upon by the defense and prosecuting attorneys was not final, however. The defense attorney still had to persuade the defendant to accept it (an issue to be discussed in chapter 7). And generally a judge had to agree to the disposition as well. For example, the D.A. might agree to reduce a mandatory felony charge to an optional felony charge, thus giving the judge more discretion in sentencing, but it was still up to the judge to indicate to the defense how that discretion was likely to be exercised.

In this chapter I present the disposition process for "serious" cases. The first section describes cases involving the same offenses discussed in chapter 5, but shows how the offenses were handled differently where there was the likelihood of a severe sentence. This section also outlines the basic pattern for disposition of "serious" cases. The following sections present case materials for the typically "serious" offenses of robbery, rape and child molestation, opiates, and murder.

"Serious" Cases Involving Offenses Which
Typically Were "Light"

Offenses which, in their typical forms, were "light" could be "serious" if (1) the defendant had a bad criminal record, especially including prior felony convictions, or (2) the crime was particularly grave, showing significant criminal activity. Obviously a case involving both a bad record *and* a grave crime was very "serious," with a high chance of state prison sentence. Part of the increased seriousness was due to statutory restrictions on punishment. For example, in some cases involving mandatory felonies or defendants with prior felony convictions, judicial discretion to impose probation was limited by law. But part of the increased seriousness was due also to a judicial tendency to sentence more harshly in these cases, and to a greater interest by prosecutors in strict sentencing.

"Dead Bang" Cases

Where there was a good chance of conviction and a likelihood of a prison sentence, defense attorneys bargained explicitly to try to arrange a nontrial disposition with as lenient a sentence as possible and, at the least, an indication of no state prison. To arrange this disposition, defense attorneys emphasized any mitigating factors in the offense or in the defendant's background. Since the prosecution's case was strong in a "dead bang" case, the defense attorney had to convince the D.A. why equities of punishment called for a more lenient disposition, that is, why the case was "not really a state prison case." If the D.A. could be so convinced, then it was much easier to convince the judge, since the D.A.'s sentencing recommendation had considerable weight in a "serious" case. Some "serious" cases took little bargaining, as all parties soon conceded the mitigating factors involved; in other cases, the attorneys might negotiate for some time before agreeing on a disposition; or they might fail to agree, and then the defense attorney would probably recommend full adversary trial.

The following forgery case illustrates the explicit negotiations with a guilty plea disposition characteristic of many "serious, dead bang" cases. While the typical forgery case involved perhaps a few hundred dollars, this case was "serious" because it involved $7,000, stolen from a major oil company. The penal code did not differentiate among forgery cases in this way but, as part of the courtroom culture, everyone knew that the seriousness of a theft case increased directly with the amount of money or stolen goods involved. In this case there were twenty-two counts of forgery by credit card charged against the defendant. The prosecution's case was very strong, showing an elaborate scheme developed by the defendant to defraud the oil company. Although the circumstances of the case indicated a grave offense, the defense attorney (private) emphasized the positive aspects of the defendant's background: he had *no* previous arrests; he was black, thirty-five years old, and a college graduate; he was a licensed pharmacist; he had received an honorable discharge from the Navy; he lived with his wife and children in a nice home.

In discussion with the D.A. and later with the judge, the defense attorney also stressed that his client had already suffered a great deal from social stigma among his circle of friends as a result of his arrest. Further, the defendant still had to face administrative proceedings before a state board to determine whether he would be able to retain his pharmaceutical license. In view of these extralegal sanctions, the defense attorney argued that felony sentencing was not appropriate. The judge promised not to impose state prison, but beyond that he said the final sentence would be decided after the probation report. The defendant pled guilty to one count of forgery, with a promise by the D.A. that the remaining twenty-one counts would be dismissed.

The probation officer, impressed by the defendant's background, recommended that the defendant be placed on probation with the condition that he pay back the entire sum of $7,000 (not just the amount of the one forgery count he pled guilty to). The probation report also recommended "a brief period in local custody because of the gravity of the offense." Just before the probation and sentencing hearing, the defense attorney, D.A., and judge talked in chambers about the probation report. The D.A. supported the recommendations, while the defense attorney argued that his client should not spend *any* time in custody. The judge decided to impose some jail time, since:

> He [defendant] hasn't spent one day in jail yet. For a theft this large I think he should know what it's like in there, so I'm going to give him thirty days in county jail. He's college-educated with a good position. He should have known better.

In court the judge placed the defendant on five years of probation with the first thirty days to be spent in jail, and with the condition that he pay full restitution to the oil company. Note that this final disposition resulted in a misdemeanor sentence, as the defense attorney had urged in the early negotiations.

Questions of punishment received much more attention in "serious" cases than in "light" ones because the stakes were higher for the defendant, the D.A.s were more involved with sentencing, and leniency from judges was less certain. For example, in one assault with a deadly weapon case, the defense attorney (P.D.) pushed hard in bargaining with the D.A. to minimize his client's two prior felony convictions. The two attorneys were good friends and had developed a close, informal relationship from working in the same courtroom. As they came into the judge's chambers, the P.D. and D.A. were still arguing with each other about the disposition:

P.D.: I'm OK on this one if I can whittle down the time.

D.A.: Nope, it's ninety days.

P.D.: How about sixty?

D.A.: No, ninety.

P.D.: Sixty?

D.A.: Ninety.

P.D.: Sixty?

D.A.: Ninety.

P.D.: Sixty? [Both attorneys laughed but were still serious about the dispute.]

D.A.: Come on, Bill. I've got to have a tag on this.

P.D.: Eighty-five?

D.A.: No, ninety!

P.D.: OK, I'll go talk to my guy and see if he'll take it.

The P.D. then left the judge's chambers to confer with the defendant. The above interchange is an unusually striking example of explicit bargaining over the sentence to be imposed. The D.A. was concerned with the sentence here because of the seriousness of the case; he needed a "tag" of ninety days to show his superiors that he had not conceded too much in plea bargaining.

The P.D. returned to chambers with his client's agreement to the bargain. The judge then agreed to the negotiated sentence of ninety days in county jail, but he also indicated he would suspend proceedings to keep the conviction a felony because of the defendant's prior felony convictions. Before leaving chambers, the attorneys conversed in a jovial way:

P.D.: I'm giving you a felony conviction here, and you don't deserve it! . . . Now you owe me a favor, remember.

D.A. [smiling]: What do you mean? This morning we were talking about a year. You're lucky with what you got!

The following burglary case illustrates a process of lengthy, explicit negotiations and continuances in resolving a "serious, dead bang" case. The defendant was in custody and had five prior burglary convictions. The P.D. had continued the case once already, and he was having difficulty reaching a plea agreement with the D.A. The P.D. said that 90 percent of the time he and this D.A. agreed on "appropriate dispositions," but in this case they did not. The P.D. described the case:

> The guy was caught drilling a hole in the wall next to a safe in a store. There's no defense at all. And he's got five prior burglary convictions— and they're all good priors. I wanted to go to Greene [a judge in short cause] and plead him. Maybe we could keep him out of state prison then. In any other court it's prison for sure. The guy's just an old drunk—but Davis [the D.A.] wouldn't agree to going to Greene. And the D.A. has to consent to short cause. He figured with five priors and drilling a hole in the wall by the safe that the guy's not just an old drunk. That he's a professional burglar. I don't think so, though.

There was evidence that the defendant had been drinking just before his arrest. The divergence of the attorneys' views in this case hinged on an evaluation of the defendant's character: if he was "a professional burglar" as the D.A. claimed, then he should go to state prison; but if he was "just an old drunk," as his attorney argued, county jail would be appropriate.

Because of calendar pressure later, the D.A. *did* consent to a transfer to short cause. There the defendant pled guilty to burglary, with no indication from the judge of the likely sentence to be imposed. The P.D. explained that he did not talk with the judge about sentencing before his client pled guilty because

> we only chamberize where the D.A. and myself are in accord—we've agreed on what we want and go into chambers to tell the judge. But here in this case, there was a straight conflict between the D.A. and myself. So there's no point in talking in chambers.

The P.D.'s point here is not entirely accurate. Sometimes attorneys would chamberize with a judge even where they were in conflict; it depended upon the particular attorneys, the judge, and the nature of their conflict. The probation report came back with a generally unfavorable recommendation, as did an additional report from a ninety-day diagnostic study by the Department of Corrections, but the P.D. argued strongly for lenient consideration. Finally, the judge sentenced the defendant to one year in county jail with no credit for time served (about nine months). The P.D. commented:

Two years county jail is better than even six months of The Joint [state prison] —especially since prison might have kept him five to ten years because of his record.

In "serious" cases where the defense attorney could see no possibility of avoiding state prison, he might still recommend a nontrial disposition with some kind of bargain on the *prison sentence*. If the defendant was charged with several severe offenses, he might plead to one and thus avoid the possibility of consecutive sentences. Or, for example, if the defendant was charged with *first*-degree robbery with an allegation of great bodily injury (which carried a fifteen to life prison term), a deal could be arranged where he could plead to *second*-degree robbery (with a prison term of one to life). However, defense attorneys questioned the value of these kinds of "bargains," since judges tended to give concurrent rather than consecutive sentences even on trial convictions of multiple charges. Besides, the Adult Authority determined the final release date for defendants in prison, and it could consider the *original* facts and charges in the case, not just the charges to which the defendant pled guilty.

Similarly, the D.A. could offer to "strike the priors"—that is, offer no evidence on the defendant's prior felony convictions—in exchange for a guilty plea. But if the defendant was still going to prison, then most defense attorneys did not think this kind of offer was worth very much. According to defense attorneys, the Adult Authority would hold a defendant with "priors" much longer in prison *regardless* of whether these "priors" were formally stricken by the D.A. in a plea bargain. Thus, defense and prosecuting attorneys did not often agree on a plea bargain involving a prison sentence.

Consequently, for many "serious, dead bang" cases where the defense attorney could not successfully bargain for a "no state prison" sentence, a trial disposition was chosen. As one judge explained,

> If the defendant did what he did and he's going to prison for it anyway—particularly if it's a heinous offense—then he's not going to get any consideration from me or the probation department. *In that case, his lawyer will tell him that he can't do anything for him, so he might as well go to trial and take his chances on an acquittal* [emphasis added].

Typical cases which were likely to go to trial because "there is no room for negotiations" included (the judge continued):

> Armed robbery—that gets five to life. Forcible rape. First-degree burglary with maybe some injuries involved. Murder cases. Some child molestation cases.

"Reasonable Doubt" Cases

In "serious" cases with a chance of acquittal on the original charge (but likely conviction on a lesser charge), defense attorneys bargained explicitly to arrange a nontrial disposition on the lesser charge, with an indication of as lenient a sentence as possible. Convergence of D.A. and defense attorney views was more likely to occur in these cases than in the "dead bang" ones, because the D.A.s were more willing to compromise because of the weakness of their case. If the attorneys could not converge on an appropriate plea bargain, then the case would probably be settled by trial. But there were strong incentives for convergence in this situation, as the costs of trial were high for both parties. Prosecutors wanted to avoid trial because of the risk that they might lose the case entirely—a conviction on a lesser charge was at least a certain conviction. Defense attorneys wanted to avoid trial because of the sentencing risks of conviction on the original charge, given the gravity of the offense and/or prior record of the defendant.

In "serious" cases where there was a chance of complete acquittal, the defense attorney might recommend trial or plea bargain. In this type of case, the defense attorney's perception of the value of a plea bargain depended not only on considerations of sentence and charge, but also on whether he believed his client was in fact guilty of the offense. If the defendant admitted his guilt to his attorney, then the defense attorney would probably recommend a negotiated disposition because of the high sentencing risks of trial. But what if the defendant solidly maintained his innocence, in addition to having a chance of acquittal based on the evidence? Then any offer of a lenient sentence was unacceptable, and yet the sentencing risks of trial were high. The defense attorney's recommendation on disposition was indeterminate here because it depended so heavily on the attorney/client interaction and specific characteristics of the case. Frequently defense attorneys recommended trial in spite of the risks, but they were also likely to leave the decision more to their clients with *no* recommendation. Or, their recommendation might be based more upon their own interests, such as the attorney's time schedule or fee in the case.

The following auto theft case illustrates the difficulties in constructing a disposition strategy in a "serious, reasonable doubt" case. Although auto theft was typically a "light" offense, a defendant with several prior convictions faced a possible prison sentence. In this case the defendant, a twenty-three-year-old Mexican-American, was charged with auto theft and joy riding. The defendant said that he had been at a party, drunk, and a friend had told him he could borrow the friend's car. The defendant denied stealing the car or having any knowledge that the car was stolen. Police, however, noted that they found wires hanging in the ignition when the defendant was stopped. At first, the defense attorney (a P.D.) was planning on an adversary trial since the defendant denied any guilt and said that friends would testify on his behalf. Further, the P.D. saw no sentencing risks of trial since the defendant said he had only *one* prior joy riding conviction several years earlier. But on the morning of the trial date, the defendant said that he really didn't want a full trial, and he admitted that he was also on federal probation for car theft. The P.D. then went to the D.A. to negotiate a nontrial disposition.

The D.A. was unsure of his authority in plea bargaining as he was only working his second week in felony trials. When the P.D. approached him with the offer of a guilty plea to joy riding and a sentence promise of time served (two or three months), the D.A. said, "I can't do anything." The P.D. explained to him about chamberizing with the judge concerning the sentence, and finally the D.A. telephoned his superior, the calendar deputy D.A., for advice. The P.D. then got on the phone and talked directly to the calendar deputy D.A. After several minutes, the P.D. returned to the D.A. handling the case and said, "Seymour [the calendar deputy] has agreed to thirty days in addition to time served. He is still on the phone and will go over it with you."

At the conclusion of the phone conversation, the P.D. and D.A. went into chambers to talk to the judge. At one point the P.D. burst out of chambers and went over to the defendant (who was sitting with other defendants in custody at the side of the courtroom). The P.D. had a copy of the defendant's rap sheet (official criminal record) in his hand and waved it angrily at the defendant:

> Now I want you to give it to me and give it to me straight. What's this joy riding conviction in Norwalk? You told me that you're only doing probation for the federal conviction of smuggling, and that you had just one joy riding. Now what about it?

The defendant admitted that he was also on probation for the joy riding conviction and the P.D. returned to chambers for further discussions. The P.D. was rather frustrated at this point, realizing he was now negotiating on a case that involved the defendant's fourth car theft.

Finally the P.D. returned to the defendant with the deal that the judge would promise a four-month county jail sentence, with credit for time served. But the judge would suspend proceedings to keep the case a felony, rather than making it a misdemeanor, because of the defendant's record. In explaining the bargain to the defendant, the P.D. pointed out that the defendant could still do more time on his previous offenses since a conviction on this case meant a likely violation of probation at the state and/or federal level. Thus, even with a promise of limited county jail on this case, there was a chance of a state or federal prison sentence on the other cases. The defendant was confused and uncertain, again denying his guilt in this case. The P.D. was exasperated:

P.D.:   Look, we could go to jury trial right now on this! What do you want to do?

Deft.: What do you think? I don't know. . . . [P.D. goes over the deal again, but avoids pushing it, and talks again about going to trial.]

P.D.   [finally] : There comes a time when you have to make up your own mind.

Deft.: I just want to get out of here [jail] . If it [the bargain] means just one more month, then that's cool.

P.D.:   It's *four* months, with credit *only* for what you've done on this case. [There was some question as to how much time the defendant would receive credit for, since at one point he had been released O.R. and then did not show up in court, and was rearrested several months later.]

Deft.: I just want to get out. I want to get out of here.

In this case, the P.D. was not completely certain of the "best" disposition to recommend, because there were so many uncertainties involved. Thus, he wanted to leave the decision more to his client, but the client did not want the responsibility either. The long-range outcome of this case was not within the control of the immediate participants, since it ultimately depended on how other probation officers and judges would handle the probation violations. The case was finally settled by a *Mosley* S.O.T., with conviction on the lesser charge of joy riding, and with an explicit sentence commitment by the judge of four months county jail with credit for time served. Note how an adversary trial disposition was more difficult in this case once the defense attorney discovered his client's full record. The chance of complete acquittal at trial decreased, since the three prior car thefts would severely damage the defendant's credibility. Also, the defendant's prior record led to an increase in the sentencing risks of conviction by trial.

The next case, involving possession of marijuana and dangerous drugs, was extremely "serious" because of the large quantity of drugs involved. With over 850 pounds of marijuana and different kinds of pills, the case represented one of the largest drug arrests ever made in the county. There were two defendants involved, both represented by private attorneys. The prosecution's case against one defendant, a young woman, was overwhelmingly strong. She was caught in the act of loading a bag of drugs into a car. After this defendant's release on bail, she disappeared and the case continued without her. The other defendant, a middle-aged black man, was primarily linked to the case by the fact that he owned the car in which the drugs were found. He argued, however, that he knew nothing about the drugs and had simply loaned his car to the woman. The man had no criminal record at all. He had worked in a county civil service position for twenty-one years; he had a family and he owned his own home.

Had only a small amount of drugs been involved, the defense attorney might have been able to negotiate an S.O.T. for acquittal in the man's case. But with 850 pounds involved, no prosecutor or judge would cooperate in an informal acquittal. The case took over a year to reach trial because of numerous pretrial motions and continuances on the part of the defense. The defense attorney then recommended jury trial rather than court trial because of the large quantity of drugs involved. The attorney commented, "There's not a judge on the bench who would acquit my client." Even with a jury, there was some judge-shopping on the part of defense to obtain the most favorable judge to preside over the trial. The defense attorney knew how a judge could influence the jurors' thinking by his comments and rulings on objections. And the high stakes in the case inclined the attorney to pursue all possible adversary strategies. These defense efforts were rewarded, as the jury acquitted the defendant at the conclusion of the trial.

Robbery

Cases of robbery were routinely identified as "serious" because of the nature of the offense (a violent crime against the person) and the statutory prescriptions for punishment. Robbery involved the taking of personal property from someone against his will, by means of force or fear. Robbery was of the first degree when committed by a person armed with a deadly or dangerous weapon, or when certain aggravating conditions were involved; otherwise robbery was of the second degree. Both first- and second-degree robberies were mandatory felonies and defendants convicted of first-degree robbery were generally not eligible for probation.

In a "dead bang" robbery case, defense attorneys would negotiate explicitly with the D.A. to arrange a nontrial disposition with as lenient a sentence as possible. First-degree robberies, because of the aggravating conditions, presented the greatest obstacles to convergence on a plea bargain. But even in these cases plea bargains (with no state prison) could be arranged. The defense attorney had to convince the D.A. that, while *legally* the case might be a first-degree robbery, it was not *really* one—that is, the case did not warrant the long state prison sentence of a *real* first-degree robbery. A P.D. explained how there were two kinds of first-degree robbery cases:

> On the one hand, you have a small group of really the meanest guys. Armed robbers with absolutely the least going for them. They're really vicious. They're terrible S.O.B.s. . . . These mean ones have a back-ground going 'way back to childhood with crimes of violence. Hostile, very aggressive acts. Not usually much dope with these guys. In fact,

heroin is rarely associated with armed robbers—it's more likely with crimes of stealth. . . .

For the rest [of first-degree robbery defendants] you get a lot of amateurs. They're not really dangerous guys. Do it more out of feelings of inadequacy. Especially in the black culture, it's a very heroic gesture and a big accomplishment. But most of them aren't dangerous. Like they wouldn't pull a gun back on you. They just have the gun along. These guys have just the usual records. You know, start out with joy riding, then some burglaries, petty theft, the usual pills, and stuff like that. Weak, inadequate crimes.

I asked the P.D. how he disposed of first-degree robbery cases. He replied:

P.D.:   If it's a "real" first-degree robbery, then there's no hope of getting a plea.

L.M.M.: What do you mean by "real"?

P.D.:   A "real" first-degree robbery is one of the bad guys, the mean ones. Then it's going to be a state prison sentence. The D.A. won't give anything. So it's a flat out, no holds barred, trial. . . .

The only hope is a county jail sentence, but you can't get it on a "real" robbery. Now on the other robberies, it's different. There you can plead to second degree and get county jail, or maybe even probation.

The following case illustrates some of these considerations in the disposition of a "dead bang" first-degree robbery. The defendant (Mexican-American, in custody) was charged with armed robbery of a taxicab driver. The defendant was seventeen and he had a prior robbery conviction from juvenile court. Because of the circumstances and the defendant's age, the case was not a "real" first-degree robbery, as described above. The D.A. agreed to accept a plea to second-degree robbery, with no state prison. But the D.A. urged the defendant's commitment to the California Youth Authority, while the defense attorney (a P.D.) wanted a county jail sentence instead. The attorneys talked to the judge in chambers but, other than agreeing not to impose prison, the judge would not commit himself to a specific sentence. The defendant pled guilty to second-degree robbery. Just before the probation and sentencing hearing, the attorneys spoke to the judge again about the case. The probation report was very unfavorable to the defendant, but the P.D. felt there was still a chance for a jail sentence. The conversation in chambers below shows a very close relationship between the attorneys and the judge:

D.A.:   This guy is just seventeen but he's a really bad actor. It's a cab driver robbery. He was picked up with the lug wrench on him.

And he has a prior robbery as a juvenile. This case was sent over here from juvenile—they wouldn't touch it. He's got to be sent to C.Y.A. [California Youth Authority]. You know that's where he should go, Judge, but Bill [the P.D.] is not going to like it. . . .

P.D.:   That's right. Jail would be much better for him. Sending him to C.Y.A. wouldn't do anything. . . [the attorneys go back and forth comparing the two institutions]. Look, the [probation] report points out that he has a close relationship with his father.

D.A.:   Well, maybe it's a bad relationship!

P.D.:   He's been working, too. He had a job at the Jonathan Club [a very exclusive Los Angeles club].

Judge: Maybe that's what corrupted him. [They all laugh.]

P.D.:   He copped out, don't forget. Also, he didn't use any force until he was threatened.

Judge: You strain my credulity, Bill. I think it's a C.Y.A. matter. [More argument from both attorneys. Finally the judge agrees to a jail sentence and adds]: It's strictly for friendship that I'm doing this, Bill.

The entire conversation in chambers lasted about ten minutes, which was considerably longer than the average case discussion. In court, the judge told the defendant,

I was all set to send you to the California Youth Authority for seven years. Frankly—and I don't like to say this—you're pretty corrupt. Everything in this report says you should go to the youth authority. . . . Instead I'm placing you on three years' probation, with the first year to be spent in county jail. No credit for the 180 days served thus far. And I suspend proceedings in the case.

Later the D.A. talked to me about the case:

You know, I was right. That kid shouldn't go to county jail. He's going to get raped there so bad. They've got thirty and forty-year-old men there that are tough. In C.Y.A. they're all young toughs like him. That's where he belongs. Bill's crazy to want to send him to jail. I don't know. Bill says that there's a Chicano clique in the jail that will look out for him. The racial groups are pretty tight in the jail. And Bill says the sex thing is worse at C.Y.A. . . . *This is really what we were talking about in the judge's chambers—which place is he going to get raped the worst in?* I think he'd be a lot better off in C.Y.A. . . . [emphasis added].

This last comment is particularly revealing, showing that the D.A.'s position during the bargaining in chambers was not simply motivated by a strong punitive interest in the case, but instead was also concerned with the most appropriate sentence for the defendant. This case also illustrates the importance of the attorneys' perceptions of the correctional institutions in determining the final sentence—perceptions which were based on very limited information, much of it supplied by defendants.

Defense attorneys considered many robbery cases to be overfiled cases of grand theft person. That is, there might be sufficient evidence to prove the personal theft, but not enough to prove that the theft was accomplished by force or fear. In these "overfiled reasonable doubt" robberies, defense attorneys bargained explicitly to arrange a nontrial disposition on the lesser charge (usually grand theft person, an optional felony) with an indication of as lenient a sentence as possible. Negotiations here, as shown in the following case, focused on the weaknesses in the evidence and on the mitigating factors relevant to sentencing. In this example, the two defendants (both Mexican-American, released on their own recognizance) were charged with one count of armed robbery. One defendant was represented by a P.D. and the other by a court-appointed private attorney. When the clerk called the case on the morning of the trial date, the private attorney announced that they were ready for a three- to four-day trial. At the recess, the D.A. called the attorneys over and said,

> I'm prepared to talk disposition in this case. I'm certainly thinking of something less than robbery. Perhaps grand theft person. . . . And we might go into chambers and discuss time. I'm thinking of a county-level sentence. I'm not sure we'd gain anything by a three-day trial here.

They whispered for a few minutes and then went into the judge's chambers. The D.A. agreed to accept a guilty plea to grand theft person and the judge promised to impose a misdemeanor sentence, if the probation report was favorable.

The D.A. described the case to me and explained his considerations in making the plea bargain:

> The defendants had no aggravated involvement with the law previously. One of them had only a few drunk arrests and a conviction of disorderly conduct, a minor thing. The other defendant had one drunk driving, I think, and a possession of pills that had been dismissed. He had served in the armed forces and received an honorable discharge. He had been overseas and even got a medal of some sort. They are both employed.

> The deal was: they had been drinking heavily and were outside a bar and stopped this guy. The victim said they pulled a gun on him and demanded his money and so forth. They took his wallet, keys, and something else—some change or a watch, I think. They were caught just a . few minutes later and all the victim's belongings were in the defendants' car. But there was no gun. Now robbers don't just throw away a gun if they have one. I mean, this is something of value. And

they were caught immediately after the incident, *so the evidence on the presence of the gun is very weak. The victim had been drinking in that bar all day long and was quite drunk, so he's not that much help.* And the defendants were drunk when they were arrested—one had a .10 and the other a .18 blood alcohol reading. A person is presumed to be drunk by law when the alcohol reading is .10.

So this case is not like when some fellows march into a liquor store with a gun and hold up the store. Or a robbery of a gas station or a grocery store. I mean *this is not a classic robbery case. It's probably more of a grand theft person*—just the taking of money from a person. That's why a plea to grand theft person is very appropriate here. *We look at the background of the individuals, how much involvement they've had with the law, and the circumstances of the case* [emphasis added].

Armed robbery was a mandatory felony with punishment of five years to life in state prison and, were the armed allegation found true, the court would be restricted from granting probation; grand theft person, on the other hand, was an optional felony. Thus, although the defendants' backgrounds would call for lenient sentencing, the risks of the trial were considerable. After the defense attorneys had talked with the D.A. and chamberized with the judge, they went out into the hall to explain the plea bargain to their clients. Later I asked the P.D. if he had spoken to the D.A. earlier about possibilities for a nontrial disposition. He said,

No, they [D.A.s] came to us with a pretty good offer. We were ready to try it. But it's really a "dogmeat" case. The guys were drunk. It happened outside a bar. . . . But what got me was Hale [the private attorney]. That was just a tactic for him to announce "ready for trial," because when we got outside to talk to our clients, *he* was the one who really came down hard on the guys. He told them just how it was and that this was a damned good deal. That the risks of trial were high. . . . The problem was that the boy's mother was outside too and she kept saying, "But my son didn't do it." She finally got shut up and Hale persuaded them to cop out.

In court, the defendants withdrew their pleas of not guilty and pled guilty to grand theft person (which was stipulated by the D.A. to be "a lesser and necessarily included offense of robbery"). The D.A. took the waivers and, for the record, explained to the defendants that:

Representations have been made by the court to you that, by Penal Code Section 17, the offense will be made a misdemeanor and handled with a county-level sentence. If the probation report is not favorable and the judge decides that he cannot do this, then you may withdraw your plea of guilty.

The probation reports were favorable to both defendants. The judge made the offense a misdemeanor, by P.C. Sec. 17, and sentenced the defendants to two years' probation, with sixty days in county jail for one defendant, and thirty days for the other. The shorter sentence for the second defendant was pronounced because of his "lesser involvement in the offense," as recommended by the probation report.

In explaining the plea bargain reached in this case, one could argue for the importance of the defense "tactic" of announcing "ready for trial." While that move probably had a bearing on the dynamics of reaching agreement, I don't think it alone would account for the final plea bargain. I observed other weak robbery cases, with mitigating circumstances, which were similarly resolved with misdemeanor plea bargains, even without the defense "threat" of trial.

Defense attorneys varied in their evaluations and predictions, so that one attorney might view his client's chances differently than another would. Or, what was a "good" bargain to one defense attorney might not be to another. In the above robbery, a different defense attorney might have rated his client's chances for acquittal higher, and been less afraid of the risks of trial. In a robbery case where there was "reasonable doubt" that the defendant was guilty of *any* offense, defense attorneys faced their most difficult decisions on the choice of disposition. Here the sentencing risks of trial were high but the possible gain, complete acquittal, was considerable, and usually not obtainable through bargaining. In a "light" case defense attorneys could sometimes negotiate a nontrial disposition for acquittal where the prosecution's case was very weak. But this was virtually impossible in a "serious" case. The D.A.s would insist upon some kind of conviction, although they would also be quite willing to reduce charges and cooperate in securing a lenient sentence promise from a judge, according to the weaknesses in the case. The following robbery case illustrates the dynamics of disposition in a situation where trial posed high sentencing risks, but the defendant said he was innocent, and the defense attorney believed his client had a chance for acquittal. Other defense attorneys might have considered this to be an "overfiled reasonable doubt" case, but the attorney handling it saw a chance for complete acquittal.

The defendant was black, nineteen years old, with one prior felony conviction. He was charged with two counts of armed robbery and represented by a P.D. On the trial date, the P.D. requested a jury trial; the courtroom where the case was scheduled was too busy, so the case was transferred out to another court. Before the trial, the P.D. described the case to me:

> My guy is accused of robbery and the victims are, you know, positive that he's the guy. But I've been talking to his sister-in-law, who will testify that he was at her house the whole night that the robbery was to have occurred. And his brothers, who look just like him, will be sitting in the front row. So the jury can see them and wonder about the "positive identification."

The D.A. who had been handling the case was tied up in another trial, so he passed the case file on to a new D.A. just before the start of the trial. I walked to the courtroom with both D.A.s and listened to the first D.A. give a two-minute description of the case. I was surprised at the short amount of "preparation time" for this new D.A., but he said that was not unusual and, besides, the first day of the trial would only be used for jury selection.

The case involved the following situation: a young couple were sitting in their car one night when two men approached, one with a gun, and ordered them to leave the car. The men drove off with the car containing the woman's purse (which, admittedly, she had forgotten when she left the car). The next morning, police found the defendant, along with several others, stripping the car. The others got away, but the defendant was caught and charged with two counts of armed robbery—count 1 was for the theft of the man's car and count 2 was for the theft of the woman's purse.

After the third day of jury trial, the D.A. remarked that "it's not much of a case," and he added:

> We would have taken a plea to one count of second degree robbery with county jail time—maybe six months. Or even to grand theft person. No one was hurt. It could have been bad. But they didn't want to plead. Nelson is a tough P.D.

I asked the D.A. if he had been approached by the P.D. with any suggestions for a bargained disposition, and he said, "No." Then, several hours later, during a recess in the trial, I overheard the P.D. and D.A. talking:

> *D.A.:* ... Sure, we might go with receiving stolen property. That's clearly there.
>
> *P.D.:* What about sentencing? I'm interested in a misdemeanor sentence. Probation and county jail suspended, maybe. And that it be made a misdemeanor by Section 17. ...
>
> *D.A.:* Let's talk to the judge and tell him what we're thinking. ...

In the judge's chambers, they briefly discussed sentencing and then worked out the possible lesser offenses that would be included in the instructions to the jury (and the jury trial continued). In order to give the jury ample opportunity for compromise, there were six different verdicts possible on each count: not guilty, guilty as charged of first-degree robbery, guilty of second-degree robbery, of grand theft person, of simple assault (a misdemeanor), or of petty theft (a misdemeanor).

After thirty minutes of deliberations, the jury found the defendant guilty of first-degree robbery as charged on count 1, and not guilty of count 2. Needless to say, the P.D. was quite disappointed, and he announced he would move for a new trial at the probation and sentencing hearing. After the jurors and attorneys left the courtroom, the judge discussed the case with the clerk and myself. The judge was very disturbed that the jury had only taken thirty minutes to reach their verdict. (Note that it had taken the judge and attorneys longer than that to agree on all of the various compromise verdicts.) When asked whether the finding of first degree would mean an automatic state prison sentence for the defendant, the judge indicated that it would, as he had virtually no discretion available.

Three weeks later, at the probation and sentencing hearing, the P.D.'s motion for a new trial was denied. However, the judge then *modified* the *verdict* to find the defendant guilty of the lesser, but necessarily included, offense of grand theft person, and he sentenced the defendant to the California Youth Authority. Since the modified conviction was for an optional felony, a commitment to the youth authority made the offense a misdemeanor by sentence. Hence, the final outcome of the case was better than the risks of trial conviction had indicated. However, this outcome was considered unusual. This judge was viewed by the P.D.s as being particularly fair and conscientious; most judges would not "second guess" a jury in this way.

The P.D. was relieved at this final resolution, since he had been disturbed by the outcome of the trial and how it reflected on *his* evaluation of the case. Right after the trial, a colleague in the P.D.'s office had asked him, "How'd you do on that 'dog' you took to trial?" The P.D. described the verdict in the robbery case, adding,

> That case really bothers me—knowing that we could have had a disposition [a nontrial disposition with some kind of bargain] but the guy said he was innocent and he wanted a jury trial. *I could have come down harder on him, though, if I thought he didn't have a case at all* [emphasis added].

This last remark points to the importance of a defense attorney's *own* evaluation of a case and his willingness to encourage his client to accept that evaluation.

Rape and Child Molestation

Judges were reluctant to give lenient sentences to defendants convicted of forcible rape or child molestation ("lewd acts with child"—P.C. Sec. 288). In addition, for particularly bad sex crimes or defendants with a record of sex offenses, there was the possibility of an indeterminate commitment to the Department of Mental Hygiene as a mentally disordered sex offender (M.D.S.O.). Thus, these offenses were routinely perceived as "serious" cases. In a "dead bang" case, defense attorneys tried to negotiate a nontrial disposition, usually with a plea to a reduced charge. If the circumstances were minor and the defendant had a favorable background for sentencing, a bargain could probably be arranged. But if a defense attorney could not avoid prison or mental hygiene for his client by bargaining, then the attorney would probably recommend full trial, since the sentence would be harsh after conviction by trial *or* by plea.

"Dead bang" cases of rape and lewd acts with child were not that common, however, because of the nature of the evidence in these offenses. The prosecution's case usually rested on the testimony of the victim. The interrogation and cross-examination during a trial was a grueling and emotional experience for the woman or child victim in a sex case. Sometimes the victim would refuse to testify at the last minute, or else would break down on the stand under the intense pressure of defense questioning. Of all the different offenses tried before a full court or jury, cases of forcible rape and "other sex offenses" had the highest rate of acquittal—approximately one-half of the defendants at trial were acquitted (see table 3-3 in chapter 3). Weak points in the prosecution's case and the D.A.'s fear of losing the conviction entirely led, in some cases, to negotiated dispositions to reduced charges. But, in other cases, defense attorneys saw enough "reasonable doubt" in the evidence to recommend full trial in hopes of a complete acquittal.

Thus, cases of rape and lewd acts with child had a high rate of adversary trial dispositions because either (1) the cases were so "serious" that no bargain could be arranged to avoid a prison or mental hygiene sentence, or (2) there was enough "reasonable doubt" in the case that there was a good chance of acquittal.

For example, in one rape case, the defense attorney and his client felt that they had a strong enough case to secure an acquittal, and the case was settled by court trial. The defendant was a well-dressed black man who worked for a famous popular singer. He was released on bail and was represented by a private attorney. The defendant and victim had been friends before the incident. The defendant admitted having intercourse with her but said that the woman had consented. The woman, however, said that he had used force by threatening her with a knife and tearing her clothes off. A neighbor was called to testify for the prosecution, but then "got confused" while on the stand; it turned out that the neighbor was also a friend of the defendant, much to the anger and dismay of the victim (who had thought he would corroborate *her* testimony). At the conclusion of the trial, the judge found the defendant not guilty.

A P.D. characterized cases involving lewd acts with child in terms of their typical dispositions and expected outcomes:

Cases of 288 [lewd acts with child] are extremely serious because a person can go away for life on these. . . . *But then the cases break down into the really serious 288s and the simple 288s.* . . . In the serious 288, the defendant is likely to go M.D.S.O. That's an indeterminate sentence and could mean life imprisonment. *But if it's not going to be M.D.S.O., then it's not serious. That's the more usual 288 and we can plead to 647a* [a misdemeanor charge of annoying or molesting children] *with a promise of "no M.D.S.O."*

But at least one-half of these cases [288] *are lies on the part of the child.* For whatever reason—maybe the little girl is mad at her Uncle John because he wouldn't give her fifty cents. Or the kid just wants attention. Or else, it's pure fantasy. The cops and D.A.s screen out a lot of these, but still many get through. *Then you just have to try them.* The charges are easy to make, but they're so often phony. The problem, though, is once charged, a man may be ruined no matter what happens in court . . . [emphasis added].

The following case illustrates a typical "simple" 288 with some weak points in the case. It was settled by an S.O.T. disposition. In this instance, the S.O.T. functioned as a "minitrial" rather than a slow plea. The defendant (an older man with a heavy German accent, in custody) was represented by a P.D. The defendant had one prior felony conviction. He was arrested outside a public park restroom in a poor section of downtown. A young boy said the defendant had masturbated in front of him in the restroom. The boy sent his uncle into the restroom; the uncle said that he saw the defendant touching himself. However, the defendant said that he was merely urinating and he denied any lewd activity with the boy. The S.O.T. trial lasted about an hour with testimony from the defendant, the boy, and his uncle. The defendant was acquitted of the lewd acts charge but convicted on the lesser charge (P.C. Sec. 647a) of annoying or molesting children. In this case, the defense attorney did not think that his client had a chance of complete acquittal. Yet the defendant denied any guilt and would not agree to a guilty plea or slow plea to the reduced charge. In the S.O.T. trial, the attorneys were able to bring out the factual dispute in the case for adjudication by the judge and still avoid a full adversary trial.

Opiates

Cases of possession or sale of opiates had a high chance of a prison sentence. While judges were lenient in sentencing marijuana or pill defendants, they were harsh with defendants using "hard" drugs. Also, heroin cases were typically strong for the prosecution. Defense attorneys tried to suppress the evidence on a pretrial motion but, if unsuccessful, the evidence was usually quite damaging. Very few opiates cases presented defense with a good chance of acquittal at trial. Cases which were settled by adversary trial tended to be very "serious," very "dead bang" cases. Compared to other offenses, opiates and homicide cases had the *lowest* acquittal rate at trial, with less than 25 percent of defendants acquitted by full court or jury trial.

In the following opiates case, two defendants (both Mexican-American, in custody) were charged with possession of heroin, possession of heroin for sale, and possession of dangerous drugs. The different processes of disposition for the two defendants reflect the differences in the strength and seriousness of their cases. The case against one defendant, Zapata, was "dead bang": the police had suspected Zapata for sometime and, through an informant, they succeeded in arresting Zapata with the heroin and pills in his possession. Zapata also had five prior felony convictions. But the case against Cruz, the codefendant, was a very different matter. Cruz was simply walking down the street with Zapata when Zapata was arrested. Further, Zapata told the police that Cruz was not involved at all. Cruz had only a minor record; he was represented by a court-appointed private attorney. Had the charges against Cruz not been so severe, his case probably would have been thrown out much earlier in the process. Shortly before the trial date, Cruz's attorney argued a pretrial motion to sever his client's case from that of his codefendant, but the motion was denied. Interestingly, the other attorneys in court (D.A.s and P.D.s) later commented that the motion was a "frivolous" one and that the attorney was "incompetent." According to these regular participants in court, a motion to sever was "a waste of time," because it was so obvious that the defendant would be acquitted. Indeed, Cruz later was acquitted by an S.O.T. for not guilty.

On the day of the private attorney's motion to sever, the D.A. asked Zapata's attorney, a P.D., "Hey, Dirk, what are you going to do on that Zapata matter? You going to cop him?" Dirk (The P.D.) evaded the question, saying that he would argue pretrial motions first. He raised a 1538.5 motion to suppress the evidence and then a pretrial discovery motion to find the identity and whereabouts of the informant; both motions were denied. The P.D. then investigated sentencing alternatives and he talked with the D.A. about various nontrial dispositions. Commitment to California Rehabilitation Center was not possible because of Zapata's record (C.R.C. was quite selective with its admissions). The defendant's parole officer told the P.D. that he would write a good recommendation for the defendant but that Zapata might be returned to prison for this offense as a violation of parole. The D.A. agreed to let the case go to short cause for a nontrial disposition with conviction on count 1 (the most serious count—possession of heroin for sale), and let the defendant take his chances on the probation report. Because of the defendant's record and the fact that the police said that the defendant was a "dealer," the D.A. would not let Zapata plead to one of the lesser charges against him. The P.D. saw no better outcome for this case by trial and he decided that a disposition in short cause was probably the best to be hoped for under the circumstances. With the judge in short cause, at least the defendant might avoid prison on this offense.

The probation report recommended against state prison since, if the defendant were to return to prison, it would be better for him to go on the parole violation instead of on this new conviction. The report also said that probation was not suitable because of overlap with the supervision of the parole officer. The short cause judge followed the favorable recommendations of the probation report; the judge suspended proceedings in the case, and sentenced the defendant to summary (unsupervised) probation for two years with the first year to be spent in county jail.

Homicide

Cases involving the killing of a human being were undoubtedly the most "serious" in court. There were two degrees of murder, and two types of the lesser offense of manslaughter which might be involved in homicide cases.[1] The offense of murder required "malice aforethought," while manslaughter was the "unlawful killing of a human being without malice" (P.C. Sec. 192). Manslaughter charges could be for "voluntary" or "involuntary"; both were punishable by one to fifteen years in prison. Second-degree murder was punishable by five years' to life imprisonment, while first-degree murder was punishable (in 1970) by life imprisonment or death.

Prosecutors initially filed almost all homicide cases with the highest charge of first-degree murder, regardless of the circumstances of the killing. This was done on the grounds that evidence might be uncovered later to show malice and premeditation. Also, D.A.s anticipated that many homicide cases would go to full trial and a first-degree murder charge would "give the jury room for a compromise verdict" (in the words of one D.A.). Similarly, D.A.s would ask for the death penalty (instead of life imprisonment) in some cases simply to give jurors more leeway in their verdict. Defense attorneys argued that by filing first-degree murder charges and seeking the death penalty (even where it was unlikely to be imposed), the D.A.s improved their bargaining position, since a trial would involve tremendously high sentencing risks.

Because of the high risks of trial on a first-degree murder charge, defense attorneys usually tried to settle these cases by explicit negotiation, with a plea to a reduced charge. If the prosecution's case was very weak and there were mitigating circumstances, defense attorneys would also seek a sentence bargain to keep the defendant out of prison. Of all convicted defendants initially charged with homicide (in 1970), 66.1 percent were convicted of a lesser charge (table 4-1, chapter 4). Further, 43.7 percent of the convicted homicide defendants were sentenced to other than state prison (table 3-2, chapter 3). But while plea bargains could be arranged in murder cases, convergence between D.A. and defense attorneys was less likely here than with any other offense. Thus, more homicide cases (36.1 percent of all homicides in 1970) were settled by full court or jury trial than were any other type of case. Two cases with first-degree murder charges are presented below. The first case was settled by jury trial and the second case by plea bargaining.

In the first case, the defendant (twenty-two years old, black, in custody) was charged with the premeditated murder of his stepfather. According to the D.A., the defendant had told friends that he was going to shoot his stepfather. Then he went to San Francisco, got a gun, and returned to his stepfather's house with a friend. Apparently there was a scuffle and the defendant and his friend shot the stepfather four times, with several shots in the head. The D.A. described the case to me during the trial:

> Now they [defense] claim it was self-defense—that the stepfather had a gun and started to shoot first. But, look, the guy was walking away, turned around, and the defendant here shoots him in the head, from the back. Now that's not exactly self-defense! But even if the guy had the gun and they can show that the initial shot was self-defense, still the defendant comes in and shoots him again. And then there was a third shot too and the guy is lying on the floor dying at this point. Finally, the defendant's friend, who was also in the room, was given the gun and he fires a fourth shot. That was the shot that killed him. And the friend says that it was on the express order of the defendant.

Both the defendant and his friend were initially prosecuted for the murder, but the charges had been dismissed at the preliminary hearings for insufficient evidence. The prosecution then refiled the case against the "most culpable one" and signed an agreement promising immunity to the friend in exchange for his testimony. The friend then became the main witness for the prosecution.

The prosecution was seeking the death penalty in the case, "to give the jury something to compromise with," according to the D.A. The D.A. described his own view of the case:

> *This really isn't a capital case.* The kid doesn't belong on Death Row. He's only twenty-two years old. Oh, *legally, it's first-degree murder all right, but there are a lot of equities involved.* The victim was a very bad guy. You know, he wasn't the kind of guy you'd take home to mother. In fact [laughing], you wouldn't want him near your mother 'cause he'd probably beat her up! He was a wife beater. There's testimony to it. He beat her in the stomach. The son watched him beat her . . . so we've got problems there in sentencing. I don't think it's a capital case. *It's more like a second degree, with five to life. He shouldn't get the death penalty for this* [emphasis added].

This comment illustrates an important aspect of the bargaining process in the most "serious" cases. To arrange a plea bargain in these cases, the defense attorney's views must converge with those of superiors in the prosecution's office, not just with the individual prosecutor involved. In this example, the D.A. felt that the case was *really* "more like a second-degree" case because the punishment for second degree was more appropriate for the circumstances, even though the defendant was *legally* guilty of first-degree murder. Had the case involved a lesser offense, it probably would have been settled by nontrial disposition to second degree, since this was the D.A.'s view of the case. However, this D.A. did not have full discretion in handling the case and he was constrained by the superiors in his office from accepting the plea bargain (to second degree) suggested by the defense attorney. Also, the D.A. was directed to seek the death penalty even though he did not personally feel that it was appropriate for the case. I asked the D.A.,

L.M.M.:   Why are you seeking the death penalty if you don't think it's "a death penalty case"?

D.A.:   My boss told me to.

L.M.M.:   Who is that?

D.A.:   Adams. He's chief of central operations here. . . . You know, *a D.A. doesn't have to try a death penalty case unless he wants to.* If Adams said definitely, "I want the death penalty on this," I could have said, "OK, but I won't try it." And then they would get somebody else to try it. You don't have to do it. *Of course* [laughing], *it's not too wise 'cause then you're bound to get a pretty bad recommendation from your superior . . .* [emphasis added].

In a similar vein, the D.A. explained to me what happened before the trial, as he and the P.D. attempted to negotiate a disposition in the case.

D.A.:   We had an offer from Garber, the P.D. in this case, for a plea to second degree. I think that's just what it's worth. Probably the jury is going to come back with second degree, or even manslaughter, because of the equities involved.

L.M.M.:   Why didn't you take the plea to second degree?

D.A.:   I went to Adams with it. He's the one who has to OK it but he turned it down. I argued with him. In fact, I went to him three times with David's [the P.D.] offer. But the only thing he [Adams] said was to come back and offer first degree and life.

L.M.M.:   Did you tell that to David?

D.A.:   Yeah, but he turned it down. I would have, too. It's a bad deal. After all, first and life, the first chance at parole would be seven years. With second degree—which is five to life—the chance at parole is after three years. By going to jury, he's not going to get the death penalty anyway. Besides, he might even get an acquittal, so you know, why not try it? A private attorney might have taken the deal [first and life] —he wouldn't be able to spend the time in trial that the public defender can. The public defender is on salary and he can spend the time on this sort of thing. So he wouldn't take it [the deal].

At the conclusion of the trial, the jury found the defendant guilty of voluntary manslaughter. Later, in the P.D. coffee room, several P.D.s praised the performance of their colleague. As one P.D. said, "That case . . . was really something. Getting a jury to go voluntary manslaughter on it. I mean, that was a good first-degree murder if I ever saw one!"

The P.D.s also noted that the D.A. had not done a very good job arguing the case at trial; the D.A. was "a nice guy," they said, but he seemed to be on a losing streak with jury trials.

In the next homicide, the prosecution's case was very weak, and the charge of first-degree murder was clearly overfiled for the circumstances. There were also many "equities" involved that would call for lenient punishment if the defendant were convicted. The defendant, Mrs. Simmons, was fifty-one years old and in very poor health. She had been released on her own recognizance. She received disability payments on welfare and, for the past ten years, lived with her boyfriend, the victim. The situation in the case was first presented to the judge in a 995 motion to quash the information for insufficient evidence. Her attorney (P.D.) summarized the facts based upon the transcript of the preliminary hearing:

> *There is no indication here of malice, or of any willfulness or premeditation.* It is not a first- or second-degree murder. . . . Here we have testimony to repeated threats from the victim to my client. The victim had been drinking and he had an iron bar and then a gun. . . . They were arguing and there was a struggle. The gun discharges and the victim is shot. Immediately my client runs for an ambulance. . . . There is no consciousness of guilt or intent to kill by the defendant. Therefore, *the elements of murder or voluntary manslaughter are not present.*
>
> Further, in view of . . . [the P.D. then quotes three recent appellate cases] the defendant's statements of self-defense must be taken as evidence in the absence of other information. . . . *This is an accidental shooting. At best it is involuntary manslaughter.* If Your Honor does not wish to dismiss the case, would you please direct the D.A. to file an amended information charging involuntary manslaughter [emphasis added].

Throughout the P.D.'s argument, the defendant was sobbing and another woman was trying to comfort her. The defendant was a very small, frail-looking woman, obviously frightened by the entire proceeding and its possible consequences. The D.A. offered a short rebuttal argument, pointing out that the iron bar was not immediately found at the scene (which weakened the defendant's claim of self-defense). The P.D. responded by pointing to other testimony that the iron bar *had* been found. The judge then called both attorneys to the bench and they all whispered for several minutes. At the conclusion of the hearing, the judge denied the motion but indicated, for the record, that the evidence was insufficient to support a first-degree murder charge. The P.D. then announced they were ready for a jury trial, with five witnesses present in court. The court was tied up with other cases, so the judge suggested transferring the case to an available courtroom. The D.A. complained that he had other cases to try that morning and he asked for a continuance. The P.D. objected to the delay and the judge decided to check on courtroom availability and pass over the case until after the morning recess.

During the recess another D.A. in court came over to the P.D. and said,

> *D.A.:* Hey . . . did anyone talk to you about [a plea to] involuntary on this Simmons case?
>
> *P.D.:* Yeah, we don't want it.
>
> *D.A.:* Not even involuntary and fixed time?
>
> *P.D.:* Nope. We'll take the risk. She's O.R. now. We want no time.
>
> *D.A.:* That's some risk, you know. The jury could convict on second degree.

I could not hear the rest of their conversation; they talked perhaps five or ten minutes. When court resumed, the judge called the Simmons matter again. The attorneys agreed to continue the case four days for the trial. The defense witnesses were told to return to court at that time.

When court recessed for lunch, I asked the P.D. about the case as he was preparing to leave the courtroom.

> *L.M.M.:* Did they offer you a plea to involuntary?
>
> *P.D.:* Yeah, but I don't want it. I don't think she's guilty of anything. It's [trial] a big risk. But I want an acquittal.

The D.A. handling the case could hear the P.D. talking and came toward us. The P.D. added (smiling toward the D.A.), "But this lazy D.A. here doesn't want to try it." The two attorneys began talking to each other, both looking over the pages of the preliminary hearing transcript. At one point the D.A. asked,

> *D.A.:* Why don't you go for involuntary and let the judge sentence her? You heard what he said about the case. The judge didn't think much of it.
>
> *P.D.* [after a bit of hesitation]: If she were convicted of involuntary by a court or jury, what do you think her sentence would be?
>
> *D.A.:* What do you think? What do you want?
>
> *P.D.:* She's got no record except for a prostitution rap over ten years ago.

D.A.: How about a year?

P.D.: You're crazy. I want her acquitted.

D.A.: What are you talking about? She killed someone. She killed this man.

The attorneys continued to discuss the case, examining possible nontrial dispositions and arguing over each factual and legal issue. They debated the following points (among others):

1. How much evidence was there pertaining to the victim's threats to the defendant? For example, the P.D. noted that the defendant previously had reported the victim to the police for his "abusive behavior" and beating her. The D.A. countered that she had refused to sign a complaint at the police station, however.
2. Where was the iron bar which defendant claimed the victim had threatened her with? Who found it and where was it found?
3. What was the nature of the evidence on the struggle and discharge of the gun? For example, the ambulance driver had described powder burns on the victim (indicating closeness of the struggle—which supported the defense claim that there was no intent by the defendant to shoot). But the D.A. said that testimony would not be admissible because the ambulance driver was not qualified to describe powder burns since he was not an "expert" on them.
4. The P.D. pointed to the "sloppy" police work in the case. The victim lived for six days after being shot. In fact, he died at home after leaving the hospital. Why didn't the police ever interview him during that time? Apparently the defendant was initially charged with assault with a deadly weapon. After the victim died, the D.A. refiled a charge of murder.

Toward the end of their discussion, the P.D. was fairly quiet as the D.A. began to push hard for a nontrial disposition. The D.A. said, "I don't want to go to trial on this. I've never done a murder jury trial. I really have to prepare. . . . Look up cases, procedures . . . like how to voir dire the jury. Look, what do you want?" The P.D. then indicated, "You check with Seymour [the calendar deputy D.A. for the courtroom] and see what he'll give. You have to talk to him, don't you?" There were three D.A.s assigned to this courtroom. The P.D. knew that Roberts, the D.A. handling the case, was new and had little authority,[2] while either Seymour or Thorn [the third D.A.] would be able to reach a bargain in the case. Thorn was in the court at the time, talking to the clerk. Roberts went to him for help in the negotiations, and Thorn finished the discussion with the P.D.:

D.A. Roberts   [to Thorn]: What sentence do you think she should get?

D.A. Thorn: Ummm. Nine months, maybe.

P.D.:   Oh, come on. . . .

D.A. Thorn: How much time did she do? [referring to her time in custody before she was released O.R.].

P.D.:   Three weeks.

D.A. Thorn: How about a misdemeanor? [that is, a misdemeanor sentence].

P.D.:   We can't do it on a manslaughter charge.

D.A. Thorn: Then, proceedings suspended with a long term of probation? . . . Thirty days' county jail on top of what she's done?

P.D.   [silent but nodding some approval]: Perhaps. . . .

The P.D. was satisfied with this sentence, and discussion shifted to whether they could get the judge to agree to it. The judge was new on the bench and none of the attorneys seemed to know him very well. The attorneys decided to talk to the judge in chambers right then to see if he would commit himself to their agreed-upon sentence (of thirty days' jail).

The next morning I spoke to the P.D. about the case and asked if the judge had agreed to their bargain. The P.D. said:

> He [the judge] admitted he was new, but said that he trusted the D.A.'s judgment in the matter. Finally he said that he thought that thirty days would "sit comfortably" with him. Ha! He said that he was going to talk to a few other judges to get their reaction to the deal. I sure hope he doesn't, because we've got a pretty good deal here now. . . .

> Roberts did the prelim on this Simmons case when he was over in municipal court before coming here. That's why he knows what a bad case it is and doesn't want to try it. "Two days to prepare," he said. That's a joke! It would take *me* that long, though, because I've never done a murder case. I talked to my boss [P.D. chief of felony trials] yesterday to get some advice on what to do here. He thought we had a pretty good deal. The alternative is to risk a jury conviction on second-degree murder. That would mean automatic time in the Joint. I don't know. I'll talk to Mrs. Simmons this afternoon and see what she wants to do.

The defendant was very afraid of a murder conviction. She wanted to avoid the insecurity and ordeal of trial, so she accepted the plea bargain suggested by her attorney. Several days later the judge decided that he wasn't sure he could commit himself to the thirty-day sentence. After further discussion with the attorneys, the judge requested a preplea probation report on the defendant so that he would have more information on her and the offense. There was a danger of self-incrimination with this unusual type of report, so the P.D. obtained the stipulation from the D.A. and court that nothing the defendant might say to the probation officer could be used against her later. The report was very favorable to the defendant and recommended that she be placed on probation with some time in custody "in view of the gravity of the offense." After reading the report, the judge agreed to the thirty-day sentence. The defendant then changed her plea of not guilty to one of *nolo contendere* to the "lesser, necessarily included offense" of involuntary manslaughter. And the judge sentenced her as they had all agreed.

In this case the P.D. had seen a chance of acquittal for his client. The prosecution's case was very weak; that accounts for the *D.A.'s* initial offer to plea bargain instead of the usual pattern of defense initiation of the bargaining. The negotiations themselves were explicit and involved various other participants besides the D.A., the P.D., and judge handling the case; that is, others were consulted in the D.A.'s and P.D.'s offices, and even other judges were consulted by the trial judge, to obtain advice about the final plea bargain. Also, the personalities and experiences of the individual attorneys entered into the dynamics of convergence in that neither the D.A. nor the P.D. had ever done a murder jury trial before.

Conclusion

Participants considered "serious" cases to be the important ones for the court and thus deserving of the most attention. Here the stakes were high in sentencing since the defendant faced a good chance of state prison if convicted as charged. And prosecutors were actively concerned with sentencing in these cases, in contrast to their more passive role in "light" cases. Since "serious" cases usually involved mandatory felonies and/or defendants with prior felony convictions, prosecutors also exercised more control over the sentencing alternatives available to the judges.

In a "serious, dead bang" case, defense attorneys would negotiate explicitly with the D.A. to arrange a nontrial disposition, either a guilty plea or a slow plea, with as lenient a sentence as possible. If the bargaining succeeded, that is, if the attorneys' expectations of case outcome converged, then they would usually seek some kind of judicial commitment on sentencing. But if the D.A. and defense attorney could not agree on a bargain, then the case would probably be settled by a full trial. "Overfiled reasonable doubt" cases were generally settled by explicit bargaining with a guilty plea or slow plea to a reduced charge. Negotiation was more likely to be successful in these cases than in a "dead bang" case because defense attorneys could emphasize weak points in the prosecution's case, as well as mitigating factors relevant to sentencing.

"Serious, reasonable doubt" cases with a chance of complete acquittal presented defense attorneys with their most difficult decisions on disposition. Because of the gravity of the offense, or the bad record for the defendant, D.A.s would rarely dismiss charges or agree to a negotiated acquittal. Yet the sentencing risks of conviction by trial were great. The final disposition recommended by defense attorneys thus depended heavily on specific characteristics of the case and on the attorney/client interaction.

Differences in defense attorneys and D.A.s and differences in the relations between them were particularly significant in explaining how the attorneys perceived the strength and seriousness of a case and what importance they placed on different aspects of a case. These perceptions, in turn, affected the bargaining process and the ultimate convergence or divergence. Nevertheless the bargaining process itself occurred within a well-defined context of typical case outcomes—outcomes determined by D.A. office policies on reductions, judicial sentencing patterns, and sentencing recommendations by probation officers.

7

Variation Among Defense Attorneys and Defendants

In the last two chapters I have described the disposition process for various kinds of cases. Throughout this discussion I have tried to show the perspective of the prevailing defense attorney *norm* on which cases "ought" to be tried and which "ought" to be settled without trial. More specifically, the recommendations of defense attorneys on the disposition method were shown to depend upon their perceptions of the seriousness of the case, the strength of the prosecution's case, and the convergence of defense attorney and prosecutor views on expected outcomes. This chapter is concerned with the *variation* among defense attorneys on their recommendations for trial or plea bargain. The first section considers variation among public defenders, and the second section compares the behavior of public defenders with that of private defense attorneys. The final section of the chapter considers the variation among defendants in their acceptance of the disposition method recommended by defense counsel.

Public Defenders

Most P.D.s routinely recommended trial or nontrial disposition according to the norm presented in chapters 5 and 6 (see summary pattern in table 5-1, chapter 5). Most P.D.s also strongly encouraged their clients to accept the recommended disposition method, because they felt they should do "what's best for the client" rather than "just what the client wants to do." Obviously *all* P.D.s tried to do both in theory, but the reality of disposition choice forced them to lean to one position or the other. Thus, most P.D.s urged a negotiated disposition if it appeared to be in their client's best interest. Three different P.D.s expressed this view as follows (emphasis added in each comment):

> There's too much risk involved to take [some of] these cases to trial. It makes whores out of us. *We'd like to do jury trials. But that's not what's best for our clients.*

> I try to tell them [clients] what all the possibilities are, the different alternatives for disposition. I try to avoid telling clients what to do. I don't overrule them.... *Well, sometimes I go down on them a little harder. You've got to for their own good.*

> Yeah, I'll twist arms. They [some other P.D.s] kid that it's because I'm lazy. The others in the office, they'll say, "Fuck him. Give him his jury

trial if he wants it." But I won't do that. I think *it's in my clients'
interests for me to get them the best deal that I can. . . . That's what
I'm here for.* I've had some nasty, arrogant people that I've defended.
"Society" hasn't been helped by what I've done. But I figure that's not
my problem. *My job is to do what I can for my client. If you've got a
bad case and it's a loser, then it's not worth the risks of trial. You've
gotta come down hard on a client sometimes.*

Skolnick (1967:65) distinguished between two normative meanings of the
notion that an attorney "represents" a client: first, "that he accepts his client's
view of the strategy of the case" and offers advice on how to implement that
strategy and, second, "that the attorney is responsible both for strategy and
tactics." Skolnick found that defense attorneys typically accepted the latter
definition. As indicated by the quotations above, most P.D.s in this study also
accepted that view of the proper role of defense attorney. However, there was a
significant subgroup of P.D.s who were more willing to accept their clients' views
on the strategy for case disposition, and who were generally more trial-minded
than their colleagues. I refer to these P.D.s as "mavericks"; the term "maverick"
was used by one P.D. to contrast his behavior with that of the other attorneys in
the office. Between four and seven P.D.s (out of the fifty in felony trials) were
described by other P.D.s and D.A.s as being "mavericks." These P.D.s are
discussed below to compare their disposition strategy with the norm presented
in the previous chapters (cases handled by "maverick" P.D.s were omitted from
chapters 5 and 6).

Tim Parker, a P.D. who had been in the office for eight years, identified
himself as a "maverick" defense attorney. I was interviewing him about a rape
case set for trial which had just been transferred to Dept. G from Dept. I because
Dept. I was too congested to handle a jury trial. This was a very unusual transfer
because Judge Greene (in Dept. I) was considered to be the best judge (from
defense point of view) on issues of reasonable doubt. I asked Parker why he
hadn't waived jury and had a court trial before Judge Greene, and he said:

I would have. And Greene is probably the only judge that I would have
waived jury before, judging by what the other public defenders say
about him. But my client wouldn't waive jury. . . . You see, the
defendants don't understand the finesse of court-shopping, or the risks
there are with different judges, etc. They just get some bull-headed
notion and stick to it.

I then asked him, "Don't you try to explain the situation to them and talk them
into what you think is best for them?" Parker answered,

No. *And I'm kind of a maverick that way.* Among the people in our
office, I'm certainly different. I can't talk to these clients—it's frustrating and you never really do get through to them. So if they want

their jury trial, then OK, I'll give it to them. I prefer to deal with the people of the court—*I'd rather talk and argue my case with reasonable people in court, instead of arguing with my clients.* Particularly with a state prison case. . . . *Remember in talking to me that I'm a maverick.* I take probably more cases to jury trial than any of the other deputies. Well, except maybe for George Birch, Ted Peterson, and Mark Rothenberg. They do a lot of jury trials, too [emphasis added].

Later on I asked this P.D. why he was a "maverick," and Parker explained further:

Anytime there is the possibility of a state prison sentence, then I recommend jury trial. If the defendant says he wants a court trial rather than jury, then it's OK by me, as long as he understands what he's doing. *My position is, "I don't insist that a defendant do anything other than what he wants to do."* It's just like if a patient goes to a doctor and the doctor thinks maybe he should operate, but the patient doesn't want him to. Then the doctor should not operate. If the patient were to die from that operation, it should be the result of the patient's choice, not the doctor's. It's the same thing with lawyers. The client must ultimately be the one to consent to a disposition or to trial. *With many cases, I cannot say with absolute certainty that it would go one way or the other.* And since I cannot, I don't want to try to convince my client that one way is definitely preferable. I don't want a guy in state prison thinking that he was copped out by his attorney [emphasis added].

Most of the other P.D.s could not say "with absolute certainty" what the outcome of a case would be at trial. But they were more willing than the "mavericks" to play the game of predicting the costs and benefits of trial and to impress upon their clients the importance of those predictions. The "maverick" P.D.s also settled cases through bargaining, but handled a much larger proportion of their cases at full trial than did their colleagues. Sometimes, however, even the "maverick" P.D.s urged their clients to accept a bargained disposition. For example, in spite of Parker's description above of his "position" as defense attorney, he related one case to me which seemed to contradict his "maverick" viewpoint. The defendant was charged with theft by a complicated confidence game called the Jamaican Switch.[1] Parker described the case:

I've got this incredible case now of a Jamaican Switch. That's a very sophisticated deal and there are only about forty guys in all of California who do these jobs. And my man's one of them. He's on probation for one here, and he's wanted for one in San Francisco. He's been in and out of state prison for these. His record is as long as my arm. In this case the D.A. is willing to give him time served. He could walk out of jail right now! But no, my guy claims he didn't do this one. Says he's completely innocent and that it's a matter of principle with him that he won't cop out to something he claims he didn't do. Well, if we take this to jury, he's going to be put away in prison for a long time with his record. The D.A. would let him walk out right now. But the nut doesn't want to. I don't know what I'm going to do with the case.

The fact that the D.A. was willing to agree to a lenient disposition (time served) despite the defendant's record indicates that the prosecution's case was probably weak. But the P.D. did not see any chance of acquittal at trial (in part because the defendant's record would ruin his credibility as a witness). Thus, Parker urged the bargained disposition as "best" for his client, instead of automatically going for jury trial, which his client wanted to do.

Several of the "mavericks" were among the more senior members of the P.D. office. This meant they often were assigned tougher, more "serious" cases than their junior colleagues, and hence convergence in plea bargaining was less likely to occur. Mark Rothenberg, another "maverick" P.D., was mentioned by Parker as a P.D. who also did a lot of jury trials. The D.A. in Dept. J (the department where Rothenberg had most of his cases) described plea bargaining with Rothenberg:

> *Rothenberg makes such a big deal out of everything.* He's so different from Bill [the other P.D. in Dept. J]. Bill comes in and sits down with Jack [the other D.A. in Dept. J] and in ten minutes they're all disposed of—all four cases. Rothenberg had just one case this morning and he's still yelling about it. Although *Bill does get the more dealable cases, he doesn't have as much seniority as Rothenberg* [emphasis added].

The judge (an ex-D.A.) in Dept. J said that he "liked" Rothenberg because "he argues and fights with me. I like that. That's why I needle him so much. Because he fights back." But on other occasions, this judge was obviously annoyed with Rothenberg's "fighting." The judge also commented:

> *Some lawyers misconstrue their function.* For instance, some of the P.D.s. They have to protect their client's rights, but that doesn't mean they have to try for an acquittal in every case. *A lawyer has an obligation to get his client to plead, if it's appropriate* [emphasis added].

Court participants generally shared this view that the lawyer should persuade his client to plead guilty where it was "appropriate," and they sometimes criticized the "maverick" P.D.s. For example, in Dept. G, the courtroom workgroup was exasperated with their "maverick," P.D. Riley. When I first observed Dept. G, I had lunch with the clerk and asked him,

> L.M.M.: Why are there so many jury trials in this department?
>
> Clerk: It's that P.D. Riley. He takes everything to jury. And he's a grade IV, too. Been around a long time. Like this case we had on Friday. . .

The clerk then described a pill case which Riley had taken to trial. The defendant had been convicted of the felony count of possession of dangerous drugs (with a prior pills conviction) after the D.A. had offered a misdemeanor conviction and a striking of the prior (a disposition which Riley had refused). The clerk said that the defendant, a nineteen-year-old girl, was in tears at the end of the trial.

> *L.M.M.:* Had she wanted the trial?
>
> *Clerk:* She didn't know. The defendants, *they don't know what's best for them. It's up to their attorneys.*
>
> *L.M.M.:* What was Riley's reaction to the verdict?
>
> *Clerk:* He didn't care. All he could see was that *he had done a good job—you know, he argued well and all at trial.* But the problem with Riley is that *he's not practical. That's not being realistic* [emphasis added].

Others in Dept. G also found fault with Riley for not being "realistic" and they cited as an example an auto theft case which Riley was arguing in a jury trial. In this case the defendant (age twenty-six, Mexican-American, in custody) had been caught with a stolen car and charged with the alternative counts of grand theft auto and receiving stolen property. While the offense was normally considered minor, the defendant's record indicated two misdemeanor convictions for burglary, one for robbery, and a prior felony conviction for forgery (for which he did two years in prison). The defendant said that he had bought the car from a friend, and that he had no idea that it was a stolen car. The defense had no corroborating evidence, however, and the defendant's prior convictions were brought out on cross-examination to somewhat discredit his testimony. Riley had discussed nontrial disposition with the prosecutor and judge beforehand, but Riley and his client decided instead upon a jury trial. The jury found the defendant guilty of grand theft auto, the more serious of the two counts. During the trial, I talked to the judge about Riley and this case.

> *Judge:* *Riley has a particular philosophy and strategy. His view is to share all responsibility and decisions with the defendant.* You saw him in here during jury selection. He consulted with his client on every move. . . . His trials take a long time. *And he's very jury-minded.* You know, some lawyers are more disposition-oriented than others, but he's not [disposition-oriented].
>
> *L.M.M.:* Is there any way that you or anyone can speed him up? Any pressure?
>
> *Judge:* Well, he has four or five cases trailing in here now. I'm going to keep him in trial until he clears them up. He says he has cases trailing in other courtrooms, too; well, I want him to clear some of these up. . . . No, there's nothing you can do.

He's completely within his rights. But you see, *other attorneys are realistic.* They tell their clients, "This isn't dreamland. No one is going to believe that story of yours." But Riley doesn't do that. You listen to the story that the defendant will tell in this case. It's simply not believable [emphasis added].

The primary sanction against the "mavericks" was that their clients could be hurt on sentencing because of the risks taken at trial. At the conclusion of this four-day auto theft trial, the D.A. complained about Riley, "That Riley is incompetent. He doesn't know how to evaluate a case realistically. . . . And his client will suffer."

I asked the D.A. if the defendant would be sentenced more severely now and the D.A. replied:

Sure, he probably will. He got on the stand and perjured himself by making up that story. So the judge isn't going to think much of him. . . . Riley's so bad. We offered to let him plead to receiving stolen property as a misdemeanor . . . and to strike the prior. He'd probably be out of custody by now. Well, not exactly. He'd have to wait the three weeks for the probation report. And then he'd get time served [which was four months] or maybe ten days more. But now he'll be sentenced on G.T.A. [grand theft auto] with a prior. He's going to face a lot more.

But actually in this case it is difficult to say if the defendant really was hurt by having an attorney who was "not realistic." The probation report included a statement from the defendant's parole officer which said that the defendant's behavior on parole was "marginal to fair," and that he would probably be returned to prison on *any* new conviction, as a violation of parole. In this light, the P.D.'s behavior was more "realistic" and the D.A.'s offer was not so attractive. The problem is that, especially with "serious" cases, one could not ever say for certain "what the punishment would have been if. . . ." Outcomes were shaped by predictions and interactions of many participants—some of whom might not be directly involved in the case at hand (such as the parole officer in this case). What did emerge, however, was that the "mavericks," in comparison to the other P.D.s, seemed to care much less about sentence predictions, preferring to concentrate on argument over the facts and their legal implications. One of the "maverick" P.D.s said, at the end of his interview,

I can't get emotional about these guys [clients]. They're nuts. They've got to be to do the things that they do. *It doesn't matter, really, what you do for them. They keep coming back.* There are only a very few that you can really help . . . [emphasis added].

When asked, "Doesn't that depress you? How can you keep going?" the P.D. replied, "I enjoy my work. It's fun. We've got a great office here with a good, competitive spirit." And thus, the "mavericks" tried to define themselves more as "real lawyers," engaged in the adversary process, instead of client advocates in the business of sentencing.

The concept of the "maverick" defense lawyer described here involved two components: first, that the lawyer tried especially to implement the client's view on disposition strategy, a stance which led to the second point, that the lawyer was more likely to take cases to full trial. These two points generally went together with the "maverick" P.D.s in Los Angeles, but even these attorneys differed from each other, for example, in the extent to which they would recommend trial where there were high sentencing risks.[2]

Comparison of Private Attorneys with Public Defenders

Several early studies of criminal courts suggested that a crucial factor for the method of case disposition is the type of defense counsel. For instance, Silverstein (1965:53) and Oaks and Lehman (1968:157) found that private defense attorneys settled more of their cases by full trial than did public defenders. But other studies, investigating different jurisdictions, have reported little or no difference between public defenders (or other appointed counsel) and privately retained attorneys in their tendency to go to trial (Stover and Eckart 1975:272; Taylor and associates 1972:271; Taylor and associates 1973:22).

Simple statistical comparison of different disposition rates may be misleading, however, because of the fact that clients are *assigned* to the public defender rather than having personally selected him. This leads to the problem of "client-control," which "is experienced by all defense attorneys, but is exaggerated in relations between the public defender and his client" (Skolnick 1967:65). This problem is clearly shown by Levine's (1975) study of defense counsel in Brooklyn, New York. Legal Aid lawyers there advised their clients to plead guilty somewhat less frequently than did private attorneys; nevertheless, the Legal Aid clients, distrusting their assigned attorneys, chose to plead guilty almost twice as often as defendants with retained counsel (Levine 1975:226-229). A further difficulty with comparing guilty plea rates for public defenders and private attorneys lies in differences in the characteristics of their caseloads. For instance, in Los Angeles (as in many jurisdictions), significant differences were found in the offenses, pretrial custody status, prior record, and race of defendants in the caseloads of P.D.s and private attorneys (see chapter 2 for summary of differences). Finally, as Alschuler (1975:1209) notes, there is variation in the quality of P.D. offices from one jurisdiction to the next, just as there are differences among P.D.s—and among private attorneys within a single jurisdiction.

Although I do not have statistical data to do a complete analysis of the issue, the available studies of Los Angeles indicate little or no difference between

P.D.s and private attorneys in the frequency of adversary trial. Lehtinen and Smith's (1974:19) examination of all felony dispositions in Los Angeles County in 1968 shows that 8.1 percent of P.D. cases were resolved by jury or court trial, in comparison to 7.6 percent of private attorney cases.[3] And, using a sample of 2,617 burglary and robbery cases from 1970, Greenwood and associates (1976:53) found that P.D.s and private attorneys each took 8 percent of their cases to full trial.

In my interviews, however, prosecuting and defense attorneys estimated that the percentage of cases settled by full trial was *less* for private attorneys than for P.D.s. The difference between the informal perceptions and the data described above could be due to the fact that my study examined only the central district of Los Angeles while the others were for the entire county. Some participants suggested that there was a particularly high concentration of "cop-out" private attorneys practicing in the criminal court downtown, and thus the private bar compared unfavorably with the P.D.s in the central district. On the other hand, the prevailing opinion downtown that P.D.s took more of their cases to trial could simply be because P.D.s appeared at trial much more frequently than private attorneys did, due to the much larger caseload of the P.D.[4]

I found that, in general, private defense attorneys used the same factors as the P.D.s to recommend the best method for case disposition. Thus, trial or nontrial disposition depended, in part, upon predictions of case outcomes, according to the strength of the prosecution's case and the seriousness of the case. One old, experienced private attorney described how he used these factors in settling cases:

> Let me put it to you this way: what is our job as a criminal lawyer in most instances? Number one is . . . no kidding, we know the man's done it, or we feel he's done it, he may deny it, but the question is: *can they prove it?* The next thing is: *can we mitigate it?* Of course you can always find something good to say about the guy—to mitigate it. Those are the two things that are important, and that's what you do [emphasis added].

However, there was another important factor considered by private attorneys in recommending nontrial or trial disposition, and that was the attorney's own economic interest in the case. As other criminal court studies have noted (for example, Alschuler 1975:1206; Levin 1977:76-79), the fee structure for most private attorneys discourages them from settling cases by full trial. Private attorneys in Los Angeles, as elsewhere, typically would set the same fee for handling a case, whether it was settled by full trial or by guilty plea or S.O.T. Thus, there was a financial incentive to settle cases by nontrial means. As one D.A. said,

P.D.s take many more cases to jury trial than do private attorneys, because they're the only ones who can afford to. A private attorney can usually only lose money because of the time involved.

Similarly, a young private defense attorney commented,

The problem is private attorneys can't afford to go to trial too much, really. Like I set two fees—one for [nontrial] disposition and the other for trial. . . . But most attorneys won't do that. Like the other guy [a high-volume criminal law attorney] I used to work with. He'd ask a flat fee.

Besides the issue of fees for private attorneys, the problem of client-control was suggested by defense and prosecuting attorneys to explain the greater frequency of trial dispositions by P.D.s than by private attorneys. One D.A. expressed this as follows:

When a man pays money to hire an attorney, he's more likely to listen to his advice. After all, this is what he's paying for. While the P.D.s' clients won't even listen to them sometimes. So if the private attorney thinks a [nontrial] disposition would be better, he can talk to his client like a Dutch uncle. He can do a little arm twisting. But the P.D.s can't do that. They have to do what the defendant wants even if they don't think it's in his best interests.

As noted earlier, P.D.s would also "twist arms," but only to a point. Some cases went to trial as a result of disagreement between a P.D. and his client (examples of this will be presented in the following section). But a private attorney had sanctions available to make his client accept his advice on case disposition—he could threaten to withdraw from the case, or he could set an extremely high fee for trial disposition. Note that most private attorneys (like most P.D.s) believed that their role as defense attorney meant that *they* should suggest the proper strategy for settling a case, rather than implementing the strategy suggested by their client. A private attorney described this aspect of the lawyer/client relationship, using an analogy to the doctor/patient relationship. Interestingly this is the same analogy as that used by a "maverick" P.D. quoted earlier, but with an opposite conclusion:

I think this way. . . . If I go to my doctor, first of all I go to him because I have faith in him. If he tells me to take the blue pill, I guess I'll take that blue pill. It might kill me, but I'm gonna take that blue pill. . . . So, when a client starts telling you what to do, he's a dummy. The poor P.D.s, they get most of these wise guys.

While most of the regular criminal defense attorneys settled a very high percentage of their cases without trial, some of them, like the "maverick" P.D.s, were more trial-minded. These few lawyers were characterized as either respected, capable trial lawyers or incompetent obstructionists. Because of differences among these lawyers and because of the large number of different courtrooms involved, I could not tell whether—or how—these more trial-oriented lawyers were sanctioned by prosecutors or judges. There were also the "nonregular" attorneys who appeared only occasionally in court, and who were inexperienced with criminal law—often coming from primarily civil law practices. One D.A. described "the nonregulars—some just bumble around. Often they cooperate and we help them out. Some you trust and others you don't."

Some private attorneys represented indigent defendants as court-appointed attorneys, under P.C. Sec. 987a. As described in chapter 2, these attorneys were paid on an hourly basis by the court. This fee schedule gave court-appointed attorneys a financial incentive to maximize the time spent on each case disposition. Indeed, Greenwood and associates (1976:53), analyzing the sample of burglary and robbery cases mentioned earlier, found a slightly higher percentage of trial dispositions for court-appointed attorneys than for P.D.s or private attorneys. In my interviews, some participants downtown saw no particular difference in the choice of disposition method by court-appointed attorneys. But a few did suggest that court-appointed attorneys were more likely than others to recommend adversary trial disposition. For example, one D.A. commented,

> Some 987a attorneys will take cases to trial because they are getting paid by the court for their time. But the cases don't warrant a trial. Some attorneys don't do this, but others do. Even where their client wants to plead, they'll go to trial. Or, where it is a case that clearly should be disposed of, they'll go to trial for the money.

However, court-appointed attorneys who blatantly took cases to trial just "for the money" risked not being appointed in future cases. In a form letter to all 987a counsel, the supervising judge reminded the attorneys of their "responsibility . . . not to expend time needlessly . . . in a 987a case."[5]

Given the focus of my study on the method of case disposition, I have compared defense attorneys only on their tendency to go to trial. Other studies such as *Denver Law Journal* (1973), Taylor and associates (1973), Stover and Eckart (1975), Alschuler (1975), and Levine (1975) provide a detailed comparison of public defenders and private attorneys on other issues as well. Lehtinen and Smith's (1974) study deserves particular mention here since it analyzes felony dispositions in Los Angeles. The authors compared sentences for all P.D. cases and all private attorney cases in 1968, controlling for the offense, prior record, and type of disposition. They found only marginal differences in the sentences, suggesting "that it does not really matter in the actual results whether convicted offenders are represented by public defenders or private attorneys" (Lehtinen and Smith 1974:17).[6]

Defendants

Throughout this discussion of case disposition, I have concentrated on the defense attorney's recommendation on disposition method. But the final decision to plead guilty or go to trial belongs to the defendant, not to his attorney. As one P.D. said,

> You know, the D.A.s can holler all they want about what fools we are sometimes to turn down their deals. But you gotta remember that we've got our clients to answer to. We're not free agents in this thing, like the D.A.s are.

And another P.D. was discussing characteristics of a "triable case" and then added, "But look, for defense, if a guy wants to go to trial, you've got to go to trial!" However, as indicated earlier, this last comment was somewhat more applicable to the P.D.s than to private attorneys. Clients of private attorneys were more likely than P.D. clients to accept their attorneys' advice on disposition.

Some cases went to trial because of disagreement between the defendant and his attorney, not because of disagreement between the defense attorney and the D.A. For example, a P.D. described such a case:

> The defendant was black and had been living in Hollywood, trying to make that scene up there, but not completely in it. He had no record at all. He was charged with kidnapping and two counts . . . forcible rape and forcible oral copulation. The charges looked bad but by the circumstances it wasn't really a bad case. I talked to the D.A. about it and he agreed. So we went in to talk to Judge Dawson. The D.A. explained that there really wasn't much of a case here, and agreed to let him plead to one count, and the judge would sentence him to ten months county jail.
>
> That's really a break and I went into the jail elated with it to explain it to my client. But he wouldn't take it. He was a real hard head, saying, "I ain't going to plead to no fucking white man. I didn't do it and I want a trial." The guy was crazy but I had no choice. We took it to trial. . . . And the judge found him guilty and sentenced him to three concurrent terms of one to twenty-five years in state prison.
>
> I was angry and talked to the judge. I said, "Look, before you were willing to give him ten months in county jail. Nothing has changed now. Why can't you still do that? Don't you realize that this man is being penalized just because his attorney fell short and couldn't communicate with him? He would have listened to a private attorney, but he

wouldn't listen to me," I argued. But no, the judge said that he's a hard head and is going to have to be punished.

I asked the P.D., "Was the defendant penalized, then, because he pled not guilty? Do judges penalize defendants who demand trial?" He answered,

> No, it isn't a club that they hold over you that the sentence will be worse if you don't cop out. It's just that the judges get angry at the man because he's so foolish. He still wasn't a bad man, but he was penalized for being stupid.

The P.D. did not explain this further but I could tell that the case upset him. The P.D. felt somewhat responsible for the defendant's sentence because of the poor communication he had with his client.

The next example shows another P.D. case taken to jury trial at the insistence of the defendant. The defendant, a legal secretary, was accused of stealing about $1,000 from her employer. The charges included two counts of grand theft and five counts of forgery. After the second day of trial, the D.A. complained privately, "This case shouldn't be at trial. It's a waste of time." When asked why it hadn't been settled by negotiation, the D.A. replied,

> It should have been, but the P.D. wouldn't do it. He's on salary. He doesn't care. We would have been glad to accept a guilty plea to just one count and dismiss the other six. But he wouldn't do it.

At the end of the five-day trial, the jury found the defendant not guilty of one count of grand theft, but guilty as charged on the remaining six counts. I asked the P.D. why this case had gone to trial, and he said, "She maintained the entire time that she was innocent." I asked if the defendant could have pled to just one count and the P.D. said,

> Of course. . . . We knew she'd lose before a court. But maybe she had a chance before a jury. It doesn't make any difference in sentencing before this judge. The woman will get probation probably anyway whether by plea to one count or by conviction of six counts—it doesn't matter. Remember that Jordan [the judge hearing the case] is a woman judge. And so's my client and she's married with three kids. She's never been arrested before. No record at all. Besides, she didn't take much. She's not a real thief.

About ten months later I examined the file on this case and was surprised to find that the defendant had been sentenced to state prison. A probation officer had found, on presentence investigation, that the defendant had a five-year history of forgery and larceny convictions on the East Coast and that her performance on probation for those offenses had been poor. Thus, the report recommended that probation be denied in this case. The judge had the defendant sent to the Department of Corrections for a three-month diagnostic study, and then followed the department's recommendation on commitment to prison. I returned to the P.D. on this case and he explained that the defendant had "fooled everyone" about her record ("including the D.A.s—she was released O.R. the whole time") except the probation officer, who had conducted a very thorough check. I asked the P.D., "Had you known about her record, would you have still gone for the jury trial, or would you have tried to dispose of it?" He answered,

> Oh, I would have tried to negotiate it. In fact, I tried that anyway, but she wouldn't hear of it. She was so adamant that she was innocent. But it was a dead bang case. . . . I did get the judge to consolidate the counts, so she was only being sentenced on one count. She got less that way, then. . . .

This case illustrates some of the difficulties involved for a defense attorney whose client had not been completely candid with him. In taking the case to trial, the P.D. did not think that there were any risks involved because he knew nothing of his client's record. On the other hand, the defendant probably thought she had nothing to lose by trial, since her record had not been discovered during the six months before trial and she might escape any penalty with an acquittal.

The final decision on disposition did rest with defendants so it is important to consider the basis for their decision. Other studies have suggested that certain defendant characteristics, such as pretrial custody status, prior record, and race are related to the choice of disposition method. For example, Trebach (1964) and Casper (1972) suggested that defendants in custody pending trial were more likely to plead guilty than defendants who had been released. Pretrial detention limits a defendant's ability to aid in his defense at trial and also pressures him to "cop out" to avoid the uncertainty and harsh conditions of waiting in jail. Also, Newman (1956), in an early study of plea bargaining, found that defendants with prior records were less likely than first offenders to assume an adversary posture against the prosecutor because recidivists knew the advantages which they could obtain by bargaining. Finally, Mileski (1971), in a study of lower court dispositions, found that white defendants pled guilty more often than black defendants, holding constant the nature of the offense charged. It was unclear, she said, whether the race difference in guilty pleas was the result of

> more numerous instances of innocence among black defendants, fewer opportunities for them to engage in plea bargaining, greater willingness to undertake the risks of "going for broke," an unwillingness to submit to "white man's justice," . . . or even ignorance of the fact that in the long run they might be better off pleading guilty (Mileski 1971:495).

On the other hand, in a statistical analysis of three urban courts, Eisenstein and Jacob (1977) found that defendant characteristics played an extremely small role in explaining variation in the decision to plead guilty; in their study, "defendant characteristics" were measured by "the combined effects of race, age, nature of defense attorney, bail status, and prior criminal record" (1977:182).

I did not interview defendants or do a complete analysis to compare disposition method with defendant characteristics. However, my fieldwork plus some statistical data from other studies of Los Angeles allow a few observations to be made on the defendants' choice of plea or trial. For instance, the likelihood of adversary trial in Los Angeles increased directly with a defendant's prior record. The differences were small but consistent in the study of all felony dispositions in 1970 by Greenwood and associates (1976) and in Smith's (1970) study of all dispositions in 1968 (which also controlled for variation between P.D. and private attorney cases).[7] Thus, in 1970, 9.5 percent of defendants with no record chose full trial, compared with 10.9 percent of defendants with minor record, 11.9 percent of defendants with major record, and 14.1 percent of defendants with prior prison records (Greenwood and associates 1976:42). This relationship is most likely explained by the fact that prior record was crucial for sentencing, and, as indicated earlier, defense attorneys tended to recommend trial disposition for defendants with bad records in many cases where a lenient sentence could not be arranged by bargaining. But the relationship between prior record and trial could also be due to unwillingness by defendants with records to accept their attorney's bargained dispositions, because of suspicion about the actual value of the bargain. This occurred in some instances where a defendant knew that probation officers and parole boards could consider the original charges filed rather than just the charge on which the defendant was convicted. A private attorney described such a case:

> First-degree armed robbery—five counts of it. There were fingerprints, physical evidence, and positive identification. They offered a plea to one count. That's a good deal, but my client refused to plead. It was based on his personal knowledge that the parole board was going to consider the other four counts. His view was, "I won't serve any less time if I'm convicted on one or five." . . . So I had to go to trial.

Defense attorneys said that their clients usually accepted their recommendation on the method of disposition. Thus, where a relationship is found between a personal characteristic of defendants (such as prior record) and frequency of trial disposition, it is not clear whether the explanation lies more with the attorney's recommendation or with the defendant's refusal to accept those recommendations.

Greenwood and associates (1976:48-52) analyzed the relationship between pretrial custody status and disposition method for a sample of 2,617 burglary and robbery defendants in Los Angeles in 1970. Within their sample, 16.9 percent of defendants were released O.R., 38.3 percent were released on bail, and 44.9 percent remained in jail. The study found that 11.7 percent of defendants out on their own recognizance chose jury or court trial, compared with 11.2 percent of defendants released on bail and 11.1 percent of defendants who remained in custody (Greenwood and associates 1976:49). For this sample of defendants, then, there was little difference in the frequency of trial disposition for defendants in custody and defendants who were released pending trial.

Using the same sample of defendants, Greenwood and associates (1976:56-59) also analyzed the relationship between ethnic group and disposition method. Within their sample, 48 percent of defendants were Anglo-American, 40 percent black, and 12 percent Mexican-American. They found a very large difference in the guilty plea rates: 62.4 percent of Anglo-American defendants and 56.7 percent of Mexican-American defendants pled guilty, while only 39.9 percent of black defendants did so. They note,

> Of course, the salient question, which remains unanswered, is whether the lower rate of guilty pleas among black defendants reflects a distrust of the judicial system independent of the defendants' guilt, or a greater willingness to fight their cases because of a higher proportion of unwarranted prosecutions (Greenwood and associates 1976:59).

Unfortunately, the authors did not report the rates for S.O.T., court and jury trial according to ethnic groups. It could be that black defendants used S.O.T. much more frequently, thus minimizing the implied differences in adversary trial rates. On the basis of observations and interviews for this study, no difference appeared in the recommendations by defense attorneys for disposition method according to ethnic group. But there were occasional indications of a relationship between race and a defendant's refusal to accept his attorney's recommended disposition, as, for example, in the first case described in this section. And a probation officer described "a racial bloc" that he had observed with defendants who would not admit their guilt—"among blacks, it's strongly felt for some that you don't cop out to the Man."[8]

These comments on defendants in Los Angeles are only suggestive of the factors which might influence the defendant's choice of guilty plea or adversary trial. Studies of other jurisdictions have reported widespread cynicism and distrust of P.D.s by their clients (See Casper 1972; Wilkerson 1972; Levine 1975). These studies—particularly Levine's (1975)—have noted how the defendant's perception of his lawyer influences his decision to plead guilty. In view of such findings, and considering the importance of the attorney/client relationship, the viewpoint of defendants on the disposition decision should be investigated further.

8 Conclusion

A common image for the criminal justice system is one of a series of screens where designated personnel sift through cases at each stage to separate guilty persons from innocent ones and then to pronounce sentence on the guilty. One study which develops this notion in terms of systems analysis suggests that "the purpose of the criminal justice system is to sort"; thus there is a criminal court "mechanism" which receives "input"—criminal defendants—and produces "output"—persons either freed, released on probation, or incarcerated (Oaks and Lehman 1968:180). My concern is with the box in the middle: to describe and explain the process by which defendants are shuffled into different case dispositions. I have suggested that a useful way to approach this task is through ethnography. That is, by a description of the court culture, we can gain a better understanding of the sorting process within the criminal courts.

Cultural description reveals the knowledge shared by regular court participants which they use to define and interpret their own behavior and the behavior of others in the court process. This cultural knowledge reflects the concepts, understandings, and informal working arrangements which have been developed to deal with the job of sorting cases—that is, the job of administering justice. To understand the criminal courts, we need to know "what everyone knows," and what is "taken for granted" by those who regularly work in the courts. Ethnography examines this shared knowledge and looks for the organizing principles underlying behavior.

> In a very real sense, the anthropologist's problem is to discover how other people create order out of what appears to him to be utter chaos (Tyler 1969:6).

My initial picture of the court process was indeed one of chaos. For example, as I sat in the courtroom, I could not distinguish between prosecuting and defense attorney. I was confused by phrases such as a *"Mosley* S.O.T.," a "dead bang case," or a "move to strike the priors." Through months of listening, observing, and questioning the regular court participants, I learned much of the language and the features of cases which were especially significant for constructing a disposition strategy. I discovered a pattern, or an implicit set of rules, for decisions on case disposition. I then tried to test this pattern by comparing it to statistical data on case disposition.[1]

In this chapter I will summarize and comment on some of the order I discovered in the Los Angeles felony courts. Additionally, the discussion will note some implications of this study and suggest issues for further research.

As attorneys examined their cases, two features were most important: the strength of the prosecution's case and the seriousness of the case. These features reflected the attorney's expectations of case outcomes in terms of the likelihood of conviction or acquittal and the severity of the sentence on conviction. Attorneys evaluated the strength of the case according to the amount and type of evidence as compared to perceived judge and jury behavior on the issue of reasonable doubt. The seriousness of a case referred to a prediction by attorneys of the severity of the sentence to be imposed on conviction. The type of offense involved and the defendant's prior criminal record were routine indicators of seriousness; more detailed information on the circumstances of the offense, the defendant's personal background, and the relationship between the defendant and the victim enabled attorneys to refine their sentencing predictions.

Court participants used these categories of cases in several ways. First, simple organizational assignments of cases to P.D.s, D.A.s, and (to an extent) judges were based on the perceived seriousness of cases, with more experienced personnel assigned to the "serious" cases. Secondly, as I showed in chapter 4, pretrial screening decisions were made according to the strength and seriousness of cases. Third, the final choice of disposition method depended, to a large extent, on these case features: a nontrial disposition (whether by guilty plea or slow plea) represented the point of convergent expectations by the prosecutor and defense attorney on strength and seriousness. Finally, whether the plea bargaining process itself was implicit or explicit was related to case categorization. Explicit negotiation, with clearly specified terms of agreement, usually characterized the plea bargaining in "serious" cases, while implicit negotiation was more common in "light" cases.

That attorneys organized their cases according to "dead bang" or "reasonable doubt" and "light" or "serious" reflected the two main tasks of the court. The criminal court must sort defendants into categories of convicted or acquitted, and the court must also sort convicted offenders into categories of appropriate punishment. Looking at court processes from the insider's point of view reveals both the importance of the question of punishment and the interrelationships between these two sorting tasks.

In the vast majority of cases the conflict between the defendant and the state was not over the issue of guilt or innocence, but it was over the issue of the punishment to be imposed. As attorneys in court evaluated the strength of their cases, they saw the results of fairly extensive police and prosecutor screening before the filing of charges. Defense attorneys would often disagree with the *level* of charge filed, but they perceived few cases with real reasonable doubt issues. In the language of the court culture, most of the cases were "dead bang" or "overfiled." But, at the same time, there were a wide variety of sentencing alternatives for each case and so the conflict between defense and prosecution shifted to the sentence. As one P.D. explained,

Most of the cases we get are pretty hopeless—really not much chance of acquittal. But often the defendant realizes that, too. The important thing to understand is that a "win" for the defense does not necessarily mean that the defendant walks home free. Instead a "win" to a burglary accused may mean petty theft with six months suspended. Or a "win" to a defendant with a long prior record may mean a year in county jail—which is the maximum time for a misdemeanor but could be a terrific break for that particular defendant.

In theory, the courts determine the issue of guilt or innocence first and *then* consider the issues involved in sentencing. But in practice it is clear that the process of determination of guilt is very much affected by the substantive effects of conviction.[2] Discretionary decisions early in the pretrial process and negotiations leading to final case disposition all reflect a simultaneous sorting over both sets of issues. Indeed, in the actual process of negotiation, participants frequently consider the question of punishment first. This is due partly to the fact that decisions about the charge are inextricably bound up with judgments about the appropriate sentence. But, even more, this reversal of the theoretical ordering of issues reflects the social reality of the court in which facts are to a large extent "negotiated matters" (Rosett and Cressey 1976:101). To discover what really happened in a case and then to determine the legal significance of the suspect's behavior is a very complex and ambiguous task. Court participants, working with uncertain and conflicting information, try to reconcile diverse moral concepts and competing values.

Further, the penal emphasis on individual rehabilitation calls for extensive negotiation over an individual's moral character as well as over the meaning of his past behavior. "Moral character is not passively established," but instead it emerges from a dynamic process of communication and interaction among various participants involved (Emerson 1969:101). In the 1920s, several authors suggested that an increase in plea negotiations (or the "compromise of criminal cases") was associated with the growth of probation and a belief in individualizing the treatment of offenders (Moley 1929; Miller 1927). And even then observers had noted a tension between the substantive goal of individual rehabilitation and a court procedure which called for sentencing issues to be discussed only after determination of legal guilt:

> It is hard to preserve a severe disinterestedness in the desirability of compromise when the conditions which make probation desirable appear early in the arraignment or even before the case comes to trial (Miller 1927:10).

One important consequence of this simultaneous consideration of the guilt and sentencing issues is that information which is only supposed to pertain to one issue may become relevant to the other. For instance, I found that when the prosecution's case was very weak, the D.A. might agree to a dismissal or a negotiated acquittal (by S.O.T.) if the case were "light," but this was unlikely in a "serious" case. Or, consider the importance of a defendant's prior record. I was particularly struck by the frequency of questions like "What's his record?" and "Any priors?" Prior record should not be relevant to a determination of legal guilt, but "everyone knew" how much prior record is important for determining appropriate treatment or punishment. Not only did information on seriousness sometimes influence discretionary decisions on legal guilt, but consideration of the strength of the evidence could also affect the prosecutor's concessions to reduce charges or agree to a more lenient sentence.

At this point I will return to my initial research question on the factors determining a plea or trial case disposition. The next section discusses the relative importance of: seriousness, strength of the prosecution's case, type of defense attorney, the defendant, and caseload congestion, in terms of the likelihood of adversary trial.

Determinants of Adversary Trial

Seriousness

The most important factor leading to a full court or jury trial was disagreement between defense and prosecution over the sentence in cases where severe punishment was likely. Where a defendant faced a good chance of state prison, because of the severity of the offense and/or a bad prior record, and where the chance of acquittal was slim, the defense attorney would negotiate to secure as lenient a sentence as possible, especially avoidance of prison. But if the prosecution's case was strong and there was little mitigating information on the defendant or the circumstances of the offense, then the prosecutor might offer few concessions toward a nontrial disposition. Hence, with divergence of prosecutor and defense views, this kind of "serious" case would likely go to trial.

The relationship between adversary trial and seriousness has been observed in other courts and explained on a similar basis as that suggested here. From the prosecutor's point of view, "serious criminals 'deserve' serious penalties, even if the prosecutor is forced to trial to obtain them" (Nimmer 1974:209).[3] And from the defense viewpoint, the defendant charged with a very serious crime "has less to lose by going to trial. He knows that if convicted he will receive a long prison term no matter what, so he is more likely to try for the acquittal" (Neubauer 1974:233). Neubauer found that the seriousness of the offense was the most important factor in which cases went to trial in "Prairie City." A related factor was a defendant's past felony conviction; the significance of both factors was linked to the severity of the penalty (Neubauer 1974:233).[4]

In cases involving typically "light" offenses and defendants with no major record, disagreement over the sentence would rarely result in adversary trial.

First, such disagreement was uncommon since prosecutors had little or no interest in the sentence, and judges tended to sentence at the misdemeanor level, with probation and no incarceration (or time served). Attorneys and judges shared a view that many of these "light" cases should have been disposed of in municipal court, rather than cluttering up the felony process in superior court. For example, the many marijuana and pill cases, and other offenses which technically could be considered felonies, simply did not deserve felony treatment. Thus, 59.3 percent of convicted defendants in Los Angeles Superior Court in 1970 were sentenced at the misdemeanor level and 49.3 percent of convicted defendants received probation without jail (see tables 3-1, 3-2, and 4-1).

Second, even with disagreement over the sentence, if there was no credible chance of acquittal, then the stakes were simply not high enough to warrant a full-fledged trial. This view was especially that of the defense attorney for whom trial in a "light, dead bang" case would be a poor use of his time. But nontrial disposition often served the defendant's interest, too, with the certainty of leniency and a faster, less public resolution of his case.

Strength of the Prosecution's Case

Disagreement between defense and prosecuting attorney over the basic question of legal guilt was another important factor leading to adversary trial. Defense attorneys would frequently recommend full trial if they saw a good chance of acquittal based upon weakness in the prosecution's case. Not all cases with pure "reasonable doubt" issues would be settled by full trial, however. Knowing the unpredictability of juries, attorneys sometimes preferred to negotiate these legal and factual issues themselves (or with a judge). If the case was not really "serious," then the negotiations might lead to dismissal of charges or an acquittal by S.O.T. But this type of negotiated acquittal was unlikely in a "serious" case. In a "serious, reasonable doubt" case, where the defense attorney saw a chance of acquittal, the case might be disposed of by guilty plea or slow plea if the high sentencing risks of trial outweighed the likelihood of complete acquittal and if the prosecutor had agreed to significant concessions toward a lenient sentence and/or charge. The choice of disposition method in this kind of case was a difficult one and it depended heavily on the specifics of the case and the defense attorney/client interaction.

Distinguishing among different kinds of "reasonable doubt" issues might help to explain when full trial would be used in these very weak cases. In using such large categories as "serious" versus "light," and "overfiled reasonable doubt" versus "reasonable doubt with a chance of acquittal," I do not mean to oversimplify the subtle gradations of seriousness and strength. Hopefully this research, as an exploratory study, will encourage others to pursue more detailed investigation into categories of cases and their relation to disposition decisions.

We also need to know more about how participants learn to identify different kinds of cases or learn "what a case is worth" in terms of seriousness.

Participants varied in their evaluations of cases and their predictions of case outcomes. I have suggested that the differences among individual attorneys were generally less important for explaining the use of adversary trial than the common factors of seriousness and strength. Nevertheless, those individual differences need to be explored as well. The next section reviews some of the variation I found in case dispositions according to the type of defense attorney and the defendant. The focus of my research was more on the defense since the defense attorney and his client made the final decision on disposition method. But their decision was made in reaction to, or in anticipation of, the prosecutor and judge's evaluations of the case. Variation among prosecutors and judges should also be investigated further (for example, see Carter 1974 for analysis of different prosecuting styles in "Vario County").

Differences in Defense Strategy

Most defense attorneys recommended adversary trial where "appropriate," according to the seriousness and strength of the case. The general norm for both public and private attorneys was to seek an acquittal where there was a good chance of it, but where there was not then the attorney should seek the disposition which would minimize his client's sentence. Variation from this norm occurred principally with "maverick" P.D.s who were more likely to take cases to full trial, and with private defense attorneys whose financial considerations would sometimes lead to nontrial disposition, even where the client's best interest might be served by trial.

A noteworthy finding of this study is the extent to which P.D.s in Los Angeles were very independent and aggressive in working for their clients' interests, rather than seeking to satisfy their peers—especially the judges. Behavior of P.D.s in Los Angeles thus contrasts, for example, with that of public defense attorneys in Pittsburgh and Minneapolis whose primary concern was "to minimize their time per case" in order to maintain good relations with judges (Levin 1977:77). But then there was a big difference between the relative autonomy of the P.D.'s office in Los Angeles and the influential position of judges over the public attorneys in Pittsburgh and Minneapolis on matters such as salary and staff increases (Levin 1977:77-79).

Defendants made the final decision on method of disposition and in some cases they would reject the recommendations of their counsel. This occurred principally with clients of the P.D. who sometimes insisted on a full-fledged trial instead of the recommended plea bargain. As discussed in the previous chapter, there was no clear pattern relating defendant's personal characteristics to their choice of adversary trial, but this issue should be investigated further.

Caseload Congestion

A common view of criminal court processes suggests that heavy case pressure, along with inadequate numbers of judges and prosecutors, is the major force behind plea bargaining. Implicit in this view is the idea that prosecutors (or judges) will make concessions to induce a guilty plea depending upon their current caseload and the time that the case would take at trial. For example, Alschuler (1968:55) quotes a Philadelphia prosecutor who says:

> The first question I ask myself in deciding what to do for a defendant who might plead guilty is, "How much time will I have to spend in the courtroom on this case?"

Quite contrary to this view, I found that decisions by prosecutors in Los Angeles were based primarily upon substantive concerns for appropriate punishment and/or an interest in obtaining a conviction. I did observe several instances in which caseload pressure on a D.A. influenced his agreement to a nontrial disposition. But on many more occasions D.A.s would refuse bargains suggested by defense and go ahead with a full trial despite the time and effort required. The relative *un*importance of case pressure in explaining plea bargaining decisions in Los Angeles is consistent with other recent criminal court studies which explicitly examine the role of case pressure on plea bargaining (Heumann 1975; Feeley 1975; Rosett and Cressey 1976; Levin 1977; Eisenstein and Jacob 1977).

A Note on Reform

My interest in doing this research was to show how an ethnographic approach to law could improve our understanding of criminal court processes. Thus my primary focus is on description and explanation of case disposition in its social and cultural context. Suggestions for plea bargaining reforms are extensively discussed and debated elsewhere. While I do not wish to comment on the larger normative debate about plea bargaining here, I do think that the major area of reform should be on the substance of the criminal law, particularly on sentencing, rather than on the procedures surrounding plea bargaining. For example, Rosett and Cressey (1976) argue quite convincingly for the legislative reduction of the statutory maximum punishment for crimes. They note that with reduced statutory severity

> discretionary decision making could then be restricted to cases in which the punishment must be adjusted to the circumstances of individual offenders in the interests of justice, rather than being used to soften the punishment of almost every criminal brought into the courthouse (Rosett and Cressey 1976:182).

But political realities dictate that such substantive criminal law reform is unlikely. Instead, issues raised by the guilty plea process are being addressed by efforts to regularize and formalize the procedures surrounding plea negotiation.

To the extent that plea bargaining reforms will focus on procedural due process, I want to comment on the *limits* of such reform based upon my observations of due process in Los Angeles. Specifically, court participants in Los Angeles were rather conscientious about adhering to due process values by means of: the routine holding of preliminary hearings; the frequency of pretrial motions on evidence; relatively aggressive representation by public defenders; an open process of plea negotiations with explicit bargains noted in the court record; and use of the preliminary hearing transcript in nontrial dispositions to provide a factual basis for the prosecution's case. But none of these aspects of the process dealt with the content of the plea negotiations—namely, the discussions of the defendant's character and the interpretation of his offense to reach decisions on the proper sentence. The effort to formalize and legalize plea negotiation "ensures that defendants are not openly told lies about the consequences of a guilty plea, but it does not ensure that the punishments they receive are either appropriate or fair" (Rosett and Cressey 1976:172).

In addition, while implementation of due process probably satisfied many of the liberal attorneys and judges in Los Angeles, the criminal defendant was left isolated by the entire process. In this sense, the felony courts in Los Angeles illustrate Abel's (1978:195) recent comment that

> the reform of the criminal law through reaffirmation of the ideal of due process tends to legitimate it in the eyes of the privileged, who rarely endure the onus of prosecution, but still disappoints the underprivileged, to whom the experience continues to appear unfair. . . .

To develop this point on the isolation of the defendant, let me suggest a few examples from my research. Then I will discuss some procedural reforms which might at least deal with the defendant's perspective.

One criticism of plea bargaining is that defendants are discouraged from challenging illegal arrests, improper interrogations, or other procedural irregularities, by the pressure to plead guilty. But in Los Angeles many of these procedural issues were argued in a separate pretrial hearing on the admissibility of evidence. Thus, there would be vigorous confrontation of attorneys in a formal courtroom proceeding and this would not jeopardize informal plea negotiations later. These pretrial motions were common because of the high number of drug cases (which presented so many search and seizure issues) and because P.D.s were particularly concerned about, and experienced in, raising these challenges. Nevertheless, such pretrial motions were often denied; the motion typically matched the defendant's word against the police officer's and judges would believe the officer. Argument over the meaning and implementation of due process (as developed by the Warren Court's decisions on criminal procedures) was a sideshow for the trial court. The conflict over procedure was really between defense lawyers and the police; having argued the issue and laid the basis for any later appeal, the defense attorney would then move on to the business of negotiating facts and determining the disposition. The defense attorney could be satisfied with his recitation on constitutional law but the defendant might be left embittered as, for example, the defendant in the "reasonable doubt" marijuana case cited in the beginning of chapter 5.

Secondly, consider the gulf between the professional and technically competent behavior of the P.D.s and the perceptions of that behavior by indigent clients. Even where a public defense lawyer was vigorously working to protect his client's "rights" or to get him the best "deal," to what extent did the defendant feel that his lawyer was effectively representing him? Casper's (1972:123-125) suggestions that we examine the adequacy of representation from the defendant's viewpoint, rather than just from legal standards, is well taken. I suspect that if felony defendants in Los Angeles were interviewed, they would show significantly more confidence and satisfaction with the performance of privately retained attorneys than with the P.D.s. Yet this would be despite very similar behavior for the two types of attorneys (and perhaps even stronger advocacy and more aggressive representation by P.D.s downtown, as discussed in chapter 7). The structural problem of clients being assigned to the P.D., rather than exercising choice in the matter, along with the lack of financial transaction between indigent defendants and their lawyers, puts the P.D. at a disadvantage, independent of the actual quality of representation he provides (see also Alschuler 1975:1242; and Casper 1972). Further, the organization of a large P.D. office according to a "zone" defense (whereby different P.D.s handle different stages of the proceedings) rather than a "one-on-one" defense (in which one P.D. would be assigned to a client through the entire felony process) aggravates the disadvantages of the P.D. in the eyes of his client.

Finally, although I was impressed by the concern of court participants in plea discussions to give defendants the benefit of the doubt and use harsh punishment only as a last resort, I found the exclusion of defendants from those discussions—and indeed the exclusion of defendants from the court culture—quite disturbing. Despite the court's ostensible focus on the "rehabilitation" of the defendant through extensive use of probation and other alternatives to incarceration, the defendant himself was seen as an outsider. In fact the use of probation was based more on the routine handling of similar kinds of cases than on any interest in the individual defendants.

If we are going to concentrate on procedural reform, then we should at least encourage reforms which might reduce the alienation and isolation of defendants in court. One small, but important, move in this direction would be to include the defendant in the plea bargaining discussions of the lawyers and judge (see Alschuler 1976:1134-1136; and Rosett and Cressey 1976:173-174). But the defendant's mere presence at the negotiations will not necessarily mean his participation, particularly when the defense attorney may see it as the attorney's responsibility to represent his client's best interests, in line with the traditional model of the lawyer-client relationship. This traditional model suggests that the client is best served by having the lawyer assume responsibility for strategies and solutions to problems brought to him by his client (Rosenthal 1974).

Rosenthal's (1974) study of lawyer-client interactions and case outcomes in personal injury cases calls into question the traditional model. He argues that more effective problem-solving may occur with a participatory model of lawyer-client relations in which clients are actively involved in the decision-making, understanding the alternative choices and risks, and sharing responsibility for decisions with their lawyer. We should investigate defense attorney-client relations in criminal law further to see which model best describes current practices and to explore whether the participatory model would lead to increased client satisfaction with both the process and case outcome. Interestingly the "maverick" P.D.s may have made a greater effort than their colleagues at full client participation in decision-making on case disposition. But the comments of the "maverick" Parker also suggested that there may have been little genuine collaboration between attorney and client, and instead the clients themselves largely controlled the decisions. As Parker said, "I can't talk to these clients—it's frustrating and you never really do get through to them. So if they want their jury trial, then OK, I'll give it to them."

Reforms to encourage greater defendant participation in attorney-client decision-making and in the larger court process must also include changes in the relationship between indigent clients and the P.D.s. Specifically, the zone defense system of the P.D.s should be abandoned in order to improve communication between defendants and their lawyers. We might also seriously consider alternative systems of providing legal defense assistance to allow indigent defendants more choice in the selection of their lawyer (see Casper 1972:124).

These changes would hopefully work to improve the fairness of court procedures in the eyes of the defendant. But attention to fairness in the substance of criminal law penalties is even more important than attempts at procedural reform.

Notes

Chapter 1
Introduction

1. See, for example, the early studies of prosecutorial discretion which suggested: that prosecutor's weakest cases would be settled by guilty plea because of the concessions which would be offered in these cases (Vetri 1964; Kaplan 1965; Alschuler 1968; White 1971); that caseload pressures were very important for prosecutors in plea negotiation (Vetri 1964; Blumberg 1967; Alschuler 1968; Cole 1970); that prosecutors compromise more with defendants who have little or no criminal record (Subin 1966; Alschuler 1968), with defendants who are free on bail (White 1971), with defendants charged with less serious offenses (White 1971; Mileski 1971), and with white rather than nonwhite defendants (Castberg 1968).

Several early studies of defense attorneys found that private attorneys settled more of their cases by trial than did public defenders (Sudnow 1965; Silverstein 1965; Oaks and Lehman 1968). But other studies have found little or no difference in the tendency to go to trial by types of defense attorney (Taylor and associates, 1972 and 1973; Stover and Eckart 1975; Alschuler 1975). Trebach (1964) and Casper (1972) suggested that defendants in custody pending trial are more likely to plead guilty than defendants who have been released. The influence of prior record (Newman 1956) and defendant's race (Mileski 1971) on guilty pleas has also been noted.

2. Eisenstein and Jacob (1977) present a multivariate analysis of the decision to plead guilty in three cities. Their analysis does show the relative significance of some of these case variables; however, it is limited by the small portion of total variance explained—only 9.2 percent in Detroit, 14.8 percent in Baltimore, and 18.5 percent in Chicago (Eisenstein and Jacob 1977:237-239).

3. See the studies mentioned in note 1 above.

4. The classic work on variation in plea bargaining processes is, of course, Newman's (1966). See also McIntyre and Lippman (1970) and Alschuler (1976). A lengthy list of studies of specific criminal courts is provided by Rosett and Cressey (1976:201-203).

5. Other recent books providing detailed empirical analysis of plea bargaining include Eisenstein and Jacob (1977), Levin (1977), and Neubauer (1974). In addition, works on plea bargaining by Utz (1978) and Heumann (1978) were published too recently to include.

6. The term "slow plea" seems to have originated in Philadelphia and Pittsburgh to refer to the brief, informal trials there before a judge, without jury. White (1971:441-442) described the "slow plea" as a trial in which "the defendant's counsel facilitates the presentation of evidence and implicitly or

explicitly admits that the defendant is guilty of some offense, but does not enter a formal plea."

7. Frake notes that these two attributes of ethnography distinguish it from stimulus-response psychology. Ethnography emphasizes mental processes, or "what is going on in people's heads," to account for social behavior. In contrast, S-R psychology accounts for behavior by examination of observable physical actions or stimuli and responses. Discussion of cognitive versus behaviorist approaches appears in psychology (Skinner 1957; cf. Chomsky 1959), in sociology (Cicourel 1964 and 1974), and in anthropology (Tyler 1969). *Behavioralism* in political science shares an empirical orientation with psychological *behaviorism*, but the behavioralist uses data on attitudes, personality, and other mental concepts in addition to data on observable behavior (Isaak 1975). Ethnography, then, can be included within behavioralism, although there are differences between ethnography and other behavioral approaches (cf. Nagel 1969), as discussed in the text below.

8. Eight of the court districts heard both civil and criminal matters. The ninth, north central (in Burbank), heard only civil cases; its criminal cases were heard in the northeast district (Pasadena).

9. Analysis of a sample of 2,617 felony theft defendants in 1970 suggested that only in the central and southwest districts were the majority of defendants black, with the central district showing 53 percent black and 12 percent Mexican-American. Over one-half of the defendants in the other six court districts were Anglo-American (Greenwood and associates 1976:58).

10. The geographic boundaries of the central district were somewhat irregular, reflecting in part the boundaries of the City of Los Angeles. Thus, for example, the central district bordered on, and excluded, the cities of Glendale, Pasadena, Monterey Park, Vernon, Inglewood, Culver City, and Beverly Hills. See Zolin (1969:16) for a map of the Los Angeles Superior Court districts.

11. In August 1972, a new nineteen-story criminal courts building was opened, and the criminal trial departments from the three older buildings were transferred there.

12. The "short cause" courts are discussed more fully in chapters 4 and 5.

13. During these two months, three different judges sat in the short cause court. This gave me an excellent opportunity to watch and listen to the communications grapevine at work among defense and prosecuting attorneys. That is, in going before a new judge, attorneys had to learn quickly about his preferences, style of chamberizing, sentencing attitudes, and so forth.

I4. There was also *intra*cultural variation. That is, defense attorneys, prosecuting attorneys, and judges, for example, emphasized different criteria in evaluating their court experiences. And even within these groups I discovered later that there was significant variation. For example, among defense attorneys, most shared a "cooperative" orientation but some had a "maverick" perspective; this distinction will be described further in chapter 7.

15. Of course, some of these "nonregulars" may have had their own "cultural scenes," or shared perception, of the court process. See, for example, Spradley (1970) and Casper (1972) on defendants.

16. I describe these changes based on other reports of the Los Angeles courts, and on a brief return visit to Los Angeles in 1976. In February 1976 I spent about two weeks updating some statistical information, observing in the new criminal courts building, and interviewing five of my old informants about changes since 1971.

Chapter 2
The Key Participants in Court

1. Court commissioners were experienced attorneys selected by the judges to serve as judges *pro tem* in certain designated proceedings of the superior court. In 1970 there were fifty-five court commissioners working full time for the Los Angeles County Superior Court (Judicial Council of California 1971).

2. The letters (and numbers) of courtrooms and the names of participants have been changed here and throughout the text.

3. After January 1971 cases were assigned directly to their trial departments at the conclusion of the preliminary hearing. Thus the role of the supervising judge was somewhat diminished, as case assignments after 1971 were generally made by the court coordinator's office. In 1974 the criminal division downtown created five master calendar departments with five or six trial departments operating out of each "mini-master calendar." This plan was abandoned after six months, however, and the criminal courts returned to the 1971 method of case assignment.

4. A new set of office policies in 1974 provided even stricter control over prosecutorial discretion in plea bargaining. Under the new policy, D.A.s were not to agree to plea bargains which included sentence commitments or representations.

5. See chapter 5 for further discussion of S.O.T. as a "slow" plea of not guilty.

6. The S.O.T. figure for 1970 is from Bureau of Criminal Statistics (1970a); the figure for 1974 is from the court coordinator's office, Los Angeles Superior Court.

7. See Platt and Pollock (1974) for discussion of career patterns of attorneys in the Alameda County public defender's office. The high turnover of P.D.s in Los Angeles is clearly explained by their analysis.

8. Findings similar to those discussed in this section on defense attorney caseload differences in Los Angeles are reported in Smith and Wendel (1968) and in Greenwood and associates (1976). Note that all of these studies (including Smith 1970) are based on countywide data rather than just on data

for the central district. I suspect that similar patterns in caseload differences would hold for the central district.

9. Unfortunately data were not available to characterize specifically defendants within the central district of Los Angeles, so information here applied to felony defendants for all of Los Angeles County. Defendants within the central district constituted close to 40 percent of the defendants in the county (in 1970); any differences between the countywide data and my informal impressions of the defendants in the central district are indicated below.

10. These percentages on age—as well as those reported below on sex, race, and existing criminal status of defendants—are based upon the total number of defendants for whom data were reported. B.C.S. (1969, 1970a) figures indicate that these data were reported for all but 2 or 3 percent of felony defendants in Los Angeles County.

11. Data are from the clerk's office, Los Angeles County Superior Court. For exact numbers of defendants charged with different offenses, see table 4-1 in chapter 4. Note that where more than one charge was filed against a defendant, "offense charged" represents the more serious one.

12. The analysis in this section is based upon data on felony defendants in 1970 from the clerk's office, Los Angeles County Superior Court.

Chapter 3
Kinds of Cases: Seriousness and Strength

1. The study of folk taxonomies is a particular concern of cognitive anthropology (sometimes referred to as the New Ethnography). Cognitive anthropology, like more traditional ethnographic approaches, investigates the native point of view, but the cognitive approach uses the native language as data, "rather than as just a tool to obtain the data" (Arnold 1976:286). For discussion of theoretical issues involved in the study of folk taxonomies, see Conklin (1962), Frake (1969a), Spradley (1970), and the collection of articles in Tyler (1969).

2. Since 1971 the entire sentencing system in California has been changed to eliminate indeterminate sentencing, setting instead standardized sentences for each offense. Under the Uniform Determinate Sentencing Act (Senate Bill 42), which became effective July 1, 1977, the trial court judge determines the length of the prison term for each convicted felon (with a reduction of up to one-third the sentence allowed for good behavior while in prison). This legislation largely codifies case law rulings by the California Supreme Court, which had already required substantial changes in California sentencing. See *San Diego Law Review* (1977) for further discussion.

3. But see Levin (1977) and Alschuler (1976) for discussion of courts in

which *judges* dominate the sentencing process. In terms of Alschuler's characterization of plea bargaining systems, Los Angeles judges were active participants, bargaining either with specific pretrial sentence promises (as in Chicago) or with "hints, indirection and cajolery" (Alschuler 1976:1092).

4. In early 1974, the district attorney of Los Angeles initiated a new policy to prohibit sentence bargaining by D.A.s. Interestingly, in the one exception allowed by the new policy, D.A.s could still agree (with prior written approval from their superior) to a sentence bargain of "no state prison." This particular sentence commitment (called a "county lid" by participants) was crucial in "serious" cases and was one of the most common bargains *before* the policy change.

5. The following discussion is not meant to be exhaustive. Instead I outline factors determining the sentence in Los Angeles, as described to me by participants, and offer some statistical support. See also Greenwood and associates (1976) for analysis of sentencing in Los Angeles.

6. The social science literature on the effect of defendant's race on sentencing is extensive. See Hagan (1974) for discussion and evaluation of many of the early studies. Note, too, how Uhlman (1977) and Eisenstein and Jacob (1977), using sophisticated statistical techniques, still come to opposite conclusions on the effect of race on sentencing.

7. But see Alschuler (1976:1086-1087) for criticism of the analysis of Jacob and Eisenstein (1975-76), an earlier version of Eisenstein and Jacob (1977). See also the statistical study of sentencing in the federal courts by Tiffany, Avichai, and Peters (1975). They found more severe penalties for those convicted by jury trial than by bench trial, controlling for the effects of crime, prior record, type of lawyer, age and race of defendant; but they did not compare the different types of trial convictions with convictions by guilty plea (Tiffany, Avichai, and Peters 1975:379-386).

8. The charge of "felony joy riding" was a violation of Vehicle Code Sec. 10851 (driving car without consent). Los Angeles attorneys referred to this charge simply as "joy riding." However, it is not to be confused with the misdemeanor charge of joy riding (P.C. Sec. 499b), which was rarely seen in superior court.

Chapter 4
Overview of the Court Process: From Arrest to Disposition

1. See Klein (1957), Trammell (1969), Meglio (1969), *Southern California Law Review* (1969), Graham and Letwin (1969 and 1971), and Greenwood and associates (1976).

2. Greenwood and associates (1976:80-96) present a detailed discussion of variation across branch offices in Los Angeles in the filing of felony complaints.

3. An even more significant D.A. policy change occurred in 1974, authorizing all optional felonies to be prosecuted as misdemeanors rather than felonies, unless aggravating conditions were present. As a result, only 29 percent of all felony arrests in 1974 were prosecuted as felony charges in contrast to the 47 percent of arrests in 1970 (Greenwood and associates 1976:124).

4. Alschuler (1968:85-86) calls these two forms of overcharging "horizontal" and "vertical" overcharging. His discussion of charging practices in ten cities (including Los Angeles) provides numerous examples and comparative data on overcharging (Alschuler 1968:85-105).

5. There are some problems of accuracy with the municipal court data reported by the Bureau of Criminal Statistics. For example, the differences between the number of felony complaints initially filed in Los Angeles (48,216) and the number of felonies filed in superior court (38,526) is 9,690. However, the sum of cases dismissed in municipal court (6,875), cases reduced to misdemeanors (2,725), and cases referred to other jurisdictions (327) is 9,927. It is not clear why these figures are not equal. See also the discussion of Greenwood and associates (1976:18-20) on this point.

6. One problem with waiting until superior court for plea bargaining was that the defendant in custody remained incarcerated an additional two months pending his final case disposition. P.D.s were aware of this problem but felt that, given present conditions, the wait was necessary for thorough investigation by the more experienced P.D.s in felony trials.

7. On the other hand, as Graham and Letwin (1971) suggest, the fact that defense evidence was rarely presented meant that magistrates were not *asked* to weigh conflicting evidence. In fact some magistrates were unaware that they even had this power. See Graham and Letwin (1971) for a very comprehensive discussion of the operation and functions of the preliminary hearing in Los Angeles.

8. In 1973 the short cause courts were renamed "waiver" courts, and court trials were also allowed there.

9. This figure is from the "Caseload Relative Weight" study, an unpublished report of the Los Angeles Superior Court, April 1971. See also Judicial Council (1971) for statewide figures on frequency of pretrial hearings.

10. See chapter 3 for discussion of difference in California between level of charge and level of conviction.

11. Only fourteen offenses are used in this table because the number of cases at adversary trial for certain offenses was too small to derive a meaningful acquittal ratio.

Chapter 5
The Dynamics of Case Disposition:
The "Light" Case

1. See Ikle (1968:117) for a general discussion of tacit and explicit negotiation. Implicit plea bargaining in Los Angeles is explained in greater detail

at the conclusion of the next section of the "dead bang" marijuana case. See also Newman (1966:60-62), Heumann (1975:526), and Church (1976:390) for discussion of implicit plea bargaining.

2. Elsewhere this kind of case has been called a "dropsy" situation. Graham (1976) notes the prevalence of "dropsy" cases throughout the country as police began to rely on this particular form of testimony to avoid the legal requirements of *Mapp* v. *Ohio* regarding seizure of evidence. See Graham (1976:135-137) for further discussion.

3. There used to be also a possibility of conviction on a lesser, misdemeanor charge, Health and Safety Code Sec. 11556. But, as discussed in chapter 2, this once-routine "deal" was prohibited by D.A. office policy in 1970.

4. Note, however, that the S.O.T. proceeding no longer functions in this way. In 1974 the district attorney of Los Angeles prohibited deputy D.A.s from using the S.O.T. to expedite a finding of not guilty. See chapter 2 for discussion of this D.A. office policy change. See also Greenwood and associates (1976:122-126).

5. Church (1976) and Alschuler (1975) also describe instances of defense attorneys taking cases to trial in response to changes in prosecutorial policy on plea bargaining.

6. Various subsections of P.C. Sec. 647 were used as reductions for 288a charges—for example, Sec. 647(a), which prohibited lewd conduct, and Sec. 647(b), which prohibited prostitution.

7. In this case, "bad checks" referred to violation of P.C. Sec. 476a, which prohibited the issuing of a check without sufficient funds and with the intent to defraud. A charge of 476a was an optional felony if the check was over $100, or if the defendant had a prior conviction on a similar charge.

Chapter 6
The Dynamics of Case Disposition:
The "Serious" Case

1. A third type of manslaughter, "vehicular manslaughter," is not included in this section. The punishment prescribed for vehicular manslaughter was significantly less than for these other types of homicide.

2. Normally more experienced D.A.s were assigned to prosecute murder cases. But this case was considered to be a "light" murder, and thus appropriate for a D.A. with less seniority and experience. Also, this D.A. had handled the preliminary hearing on the case, so he was already familiar with it.

Chapter 7
Variation among Defense Attorneys
and Defendants

1. The complex con game of "Jamaican Switch" or "Jamaican Bunco" is described in detail by the Los Angeles District Attorney's Office in a pamphlet,

"Operation on Guard: How to Protect Yourself Against Bunco Artists, Con Men, and Crimes of Violence."

2. That these two components of the "maverick" need not go together is illustrated by Levine's (1975) study of Legal Aid lawyers in Brooklyn, New York. He found that indigent defendants regularly preferred to plead guilty, even where their lawyers had recommended going to trial. The defendants' choice of guilty plea, however, was influenced by their cynicism and distrust of their assigned lawyers (Levine 1975:226-229).

3. I computed these percentages based upon the figures for court and jury trial cases, shown in table VI in Lehtinen and Smith (1974:19).

4. Taylor and associates (1973:22) suggested this reason to explain why some people in Denver believe that the P.D. there goes to trial in a higher percentage of cases than does retained counsel, in spite of the statistical evidence that the percentages are virtually the same for two types of counsel.

5. A supervising judge showed me a copy of this letter, dated March 10, 1970. The judge, who made the appointments, also noted that he kept a list of attorneys eligible for 987a work and that he crossed off the names of people he knew to be "incompetent, dishonest, or just bad attorneys."

6. For more detailed analysis, see Smith (1970), a longer version of Lehtinen and Smith (1974).

7. Smith (1970:91-92), in table XXIX, reports raw data on type of defense attorney, prior record, and type of disposition for felony dispositions in Los Angeles County Superior Court, 1968. Using the data there, I computed the following percentages of cases resolved by jury or court trial by P.D. and by private attorney, by defendants' prior criminal record:

	Public Defender			Private Attorney		
Prior Record	Number of Cases	Number of Full Trials	Percent of Cases at Trial	Number of Cases	Number of Full Trials	Percent of Cases at Trial
No prior	2,980	134	4.5%	3,865	215	5.6%
Minor prior	2,918	199	6.8%	2,543	175	6.9%
Major prior	5,419	526	9.7%	2,887	268	9.3%
Prior prison	2,957	312	10.6%	1,205	150	12.4%
No information	315	14	4.4%	313	11	3.5%
Total	14,589	1,185	8.1%	10,813	819	7.6%

8. Black defendants in Los Angeles did not necessarily fare better than Anglo-American defendants in a contested trial, however. The limited evidence from the sample of 2,617 defendants in 1970 reported by Greenwood and associates (1976:59) indicates that blacks were convicted slightly more often than Anglo-Americans in trial dispositions.

Chapter 8
Conclusion

1. Frake (1964), in defending research techniques of the "New Ethnography," suggests:

> Given two competing ethnographic statements . . . the best statement is the one which most adequately accounts for the widest range of behavior. If two statements differ in their implications for behavior, then a choice between them can only be made in one way: by testing them against the behavior of the people being described (Frake 1964:119).

2. Griffiths (1970) shows the importance of integrating process and substance in our thinking about criminal law. In an extended critique of Packer's (1968) Due Process and Crime Control models of the criminal process, Griffiths faults Packer for his limited concern with the substantive functions of criminal law. Griffiths argues forcefully "that process is affected by the whole of the substance which it is seen to implement" (1970:409).

3. Nimmer (1974:209) defines serious cases as "high priority" ones; he notes that prosecutors evaluate the "worth" of individual cases "in terms of their perceived seriousness," and this evaluation affects decisions on disposition. Nimmer suggests that this evaluation of seriousness is partially a response to limited resources in the prosecutor's office and partially an illustration of the quasi-judicial function of the prosecutor. In my analysis of seriousness I have stressed the latter meaning of it—namely, that prosecutors judge the appropriateness of punishment for different kinds of offenders and offenses.

4. Neubauer's (1974:232-234) summary of "why cases go to trial" in "Prairie City" points to almost the same factors, and the same weighting of factors, as my discussion here on the determinants of adversary trial in Los Angeles. The one additional factor mentioned by Neubauer is "credibility maintenance"—the strategic interest of attorneys on each side to maintain their credibility and improve their long-range bargaining position by occasionally calling the other side's bluff and going to trial. I did not find this factor in Los Angeles; it could well have been present but difficult to observe because of the numbers of attorneys involved.

Bibliography

Abel, Richard L. 1978. From the Editor. *Law and Society Review* 12:189.

Alschuler, Albert. 1968. The Prosecutor's Role in Plea Bargaining. *University of Chicago Law Review* 36:50.

_____. 1975. The Defense Attorney's Role in Plea Bargaining. *Yale Law Journal* 84:1179.

_____. 1976. The Trial Judge's Role in Plea Bargaining, Part I. *Columbia Law Review* 76:1059.

Arnold, Dean. 1976. New Ethnography, in David E. Hunter and Phillip Whitten, eds. *Encyclopedia of Anthropology*. New York: Harper and Row.

Balbus, Isaac D. 1973. *The Dialectics of Legal Repression: Black Rebels Before the American Criminal Courts*. New York: Russell Sage Foundation.

Banfield, Edward C., and Wilson, James Q. 1963. *City Politics*. New York: Random House.

Berger, Jesse T. 1967. *Executive Officer's Report 1967*. Los Angeles: Los Angeles County Superior Court.

Blumberg, Abraham S. 1967. *Criminal Justice*. Chicago: Quadrangle Books.

Bureau of Criminal Statistics. 1969. *Crime and Delinquency in California*. Sacramento: State of California, Department of Justice.

_____. 1970a. *Felony Defendants Disposed of in California Courts: References Tables*. Sacramento: State of California, Department of Justice.

_____. 1970b. *Crimes and Arrests: References Tables*. Sacramento: State of California, Department of Justice.

_____. 1970c. *Adult Probation: Reference Tables*. Sacramento: State of California, Department of Justice.

Carlin, Jerome. 1962. *Lawyers on Their Own*. New Brunswick, N.J.: Rutgers University Press.

Carter, Lief H. 1974. *The Limits of Order*. Lexington, Mass.: Lexington Books, D.C. Heath.

Casper, Jonathan D. 1972. *American Criminal Justice: The Defendant's Perspective*. Englewood Cliffs, N.J.: Prentice-Hall.

Castberg, Anthony D. 1968. *Prosecutorial Discretion: A Case Study*. Unpublished doctoral dissertation. Northwestern University.

Chomsky, Noam. 1959. Verbal Behavior (A Review). *Language* 35:26.

Church, Thomas. 1976. Plea Bargains, Concessions, and the Courts: Analysis of a Quasi-Experiment. *Law and Society Review* 10:377.

Cicourel, Aaron. 1964. *Method and Measurement in Sociology*. New York: Free Press of Glencoe.

_____. 1974. *Cognitive Sociology: Language and Meaning in Social Interaction*. New York: Free Press.

Cole, George F. 1970. The Decision to Prosecute. *Law and Society Review* 4:331.

_____. 1973. *Politics and the Administration of Justice.* Beverly Hills: Sage Publications.

Conklin, Harold. 1962. Lexicographical Treatment of Folk Taxonomies, in F.W. Householder and S. Saporta, eds. *Problems in Lexicography.* Bloomington: Indiana University Research Center in Anthropology, Folklore, and Linguistics.

_____. 1968. Ethnography, in David L. Sills, ed. *International Encyclopedia of the Social Sciences.* New York: Macmillan and Free Press. Volume 5.

Cook, Beverly B. 1967. *The Judicial Process in California.* Belmont, California: Dickenson Publishing Co.

Denver Law Journal. 1973. Comparison of Public Defenders' and Private Attorneys' Relationships with the Prosecution in the City of Denver. *Denver Law Journal* 50:101.

Eisenstein, James, and Jacob, Herbert. 1977. *Felony Justice: An Organizational Analysis of Criminal Courts.* Boston: Little, Brown.

Emerson, Robert M. 1969. *Judging Delinquents: Context and Process in Juvenile Court.* Chicago: Aldine.

Enker, Arnold. 1967. Perspectives on Plea Bargaining, in President's Commission of Law Enforcement and Administration of Justice. *Task Force Report: The Courts.* Washington, D.C.: Government Printing Office.

Feeley, Malcolm. 1975. The Effects of Heavy Caseloads. Paper delivered at 1975 Annual Meeting of the American Political Science Association, San Francisco, California.

Frake, Charles O. 1964. Further Discussion of Burling. *American Anthropologist* 66:119.

_____. 1969a. Notes on Queries in Ethnography, in Stephen A. Tyler, ed. *Cognitive Anthropology.* New York: Holt, Rinehart, and Winston.

_____. 1969b. A Structural Description of Subanun "Religious Behavior," in Stephen A. Tyler, ed. *Cognitive Anthropology.* New York: Holt, Rinehart, and Winston.

Goodenough, Ward. 1964. Cultural Anthropology and Linguistics, in Dell Hymes, ed. *Language in Culture and Society.* New York: Harper and Row.

Graham, Fred P. 1976. *The Due Process Revolution: The Warren Court's Impact on Criminal Law.* Rochelle Park, N.J.: Hayden Book Co.

Graham, Kenneth, and Letwin, Leon. 1969. *A Study of the Preliminary Hearing in Los Angeles.* Washington: The Institute of Criminal Law and Procedure, Georgetown University Law Center.

_____. 1971. The Preliminary Hearing in Los Angeles: Some Field Findings and Legal-Policy Observations. *U.C.L.A. Law Review* 18:636,916.

Greenwood, Peter W., and associates. 1973. *Prosecution of Adult Felony Defendants in Los Angeles County: A Policy Perspective.* Santa Monica, California: The Rand Corporation.

_____. 1976. *Prosecution of Adult Felony Defendants.* Lexington, Mass.: Lexington Books, D.C. Heath.

Griffiths, John. 1970. Ideology in Criminal Procedure or A Third "Model" of the Criminal Process. *Yale Law Journal* 79:359.

Hagan, John. 1974. Extra-Legal Attributes and Criminal Sentencing: An Assessment of a Sociological Viewpoint. *Law and Society Review* 8:357.

Heumann, Milton. 1975. A Note on Plea Bargaining and Case Pressure. *Law and Society Review* 9:515.

_____. 1978. *Plea Bargaining: The Experience of Prosecutors, Judges, and Defense Attorneys.* Chicago: University of Chicago Press.

Hitchcock, Douglas. 1972. Administrative Sentencing and Parole Decision as a Problem in Administrative Discretion: The California Sentencing System. *University of California, Davis Law Review* 5:360.

Ikle, Fred. 1968. Negotiation, in David L. Sills, ed. *International Encyclopedia of the Social Sciences.* Volume 11. New York: Macmillan and Free Press.

Isaak, Alan C. 1975. *Scope and Methods of Political Science.* Homewood, Ill.: Dorsey Press.

Jacob, Herbert, and Eisenstein, James. 1975-76. Sentences and Other Sanctions in the Criminal Courts. *Political Science Quarterly* 90:617.

Judicial Council of California. 1971. *Annual Report of the Administrative Office of the California Courts.* San Francisco: Author.

Kalven, Harry, and Zeisel, Hans. 1971. *The American Jury.* Chicago: University of Chicago Press.

Kaplan, John. 1965. The Prosecutorial Discretion: A Comment. *Northwestern Law Review* 60:174.

Klein, Richard. 1957. District Attorney's Discretion Not to Prosecute. *Los Angeles Bar Bulletin* 32:323.

Lehtinen, M., and Smith, Gerald W. 1974. The Relative Effectiveness of Public Defenders and Private Attorneys: A Comparison. *Legal Aid Briefcase* 32:12.

Levin, Martin A. 1972. Urban Politics and Judicial Behavior. *Journal of Legal Studies* 1:193.

_____. 1977. *Urban Politics and the Criminal Courts.* Chicago: University of Chicago.

Levine, James P. 1975. The Impact of "Gideon": The Performance of Public and Private Criminal Defense Lawyers. *Polity* 8:215.

McCall, George J., and Simmons, J.L. 1969. *Issues in Participant Observation: A Text and Reader.* Reading, Mass.: Addison-Wesley.

McIntyre, Donald M., and Lippman, David. 1970. Prosecutors and Early Disposition of Felony Cases. *American Bar Association Journal* 56:1154.

Mather, Lynn M. 1974a. Some Determinants of the Method of Case Disposition: Decision-Making by Public Defenders in Los Angeles. *Law and Society Review* 8:187.

_____ 1974b. The Outsider in the Courtroom: An Alternative Role for the Defense, in Herbert Jacob, ed. *The Potential for Reform of Criminal Justice.* Beverly Hills: Sage Publications.

_____. 1977. Ethnography and the Study of Trial Courts, in John A. Gardiner, ed. *Public Law and Public Policy.* New York: Praeger.

Meglio, John J. 1969. Comparative Study of the District Attorney's Office in Los Angeles and Brooklyn. *Prosecutor* 5:237.

Mileski, Maureen. 1971. Courtroom Encounters: An Observation Study of a Lower Criminal Court. *Law and Society Review* 5:473.

Miller, Justin. 1927. The Compromise of Criminal Cases. *Southern California Law Review* 1:1.

Moley, Raymond. 1929. *Politics and Criminal Prosecution.* New York: Minton, Balch and Co.

Nader, Laura, ed. 1965. The Ethnography of Law. *American Anthropologist* 67:Special Issue.

_____. 1969. *Law in Culture and Society.* Chicago: Aldine.

_____, and Yngvesson, Barbara. 1973. On Studying the Ethnography of Law and Its Consequences, in John J. Honigmann, ed. *Handbook of Social and Cultural Anthropology.* Chicago: Rand McNally.

Nagel, Stuart S. 1969. *The Legal Process from a Behavioral Perspective.* Homewood, Ill.: Dorsey Press.

Neubauer, David W. 1974. *Criminal Justice in Middle America.* Morristown, N.J.: General Learning Press.

Newman, Donald J. 1956. Pleading Guilty for Considerations: A Study of Bargain Justice. *Journal of Criminal Law, Criminology and Police Science* 46:780.

_____. 1966. *Conviction: The Determination of Guilt or Innocence without Trial.* Boston: Little, Brown.

Nimmer, Raymond T. 1974. Judicial Reform: Informal Processes and Competing Effects, in Herbert Jacob, ed. *The Potential for Reform of Criminal Justice.* Beverly Hills: Sage Publications.

Oaks, Dallin H., and Lehman, Warren. 1968. *A Criminal Justice System and the Indigent.* Chicago: University of Chicago Press.

Packer, Herbert. 1968. *The Limits of the Criminal Sanction.* Stanford: Stanford University Press.

Platt, Anthony, and Pollock, Randi. 1974. Channeling Lawyers: The Careers of Public Defenders, in Herbert Jacob, ed. *The Potential for Reform of Criminal Justice.* Beverly Hills: Sage Publications.

Rosenthal, Douglas E. 1974. *Lawyer and Client: Who's in Charge?* New York: Russell Sage.

Rosett, Arthur, and Cressey, Donald. 1976. *Justice by Consent.* Philadelphia: Lippincott.

San Diego Law Review. 1977. Senate Bill 42 and the Myth of Shortened Sentences for California Offenders: The Effects of the Uniform Determinate Sentencing Act. *San Diego Law Review* 14:1176.

Sarat, Austin. 1978. Understanding Trial Courts: A Critique of Social Science Approaches. *Judicature* 61:318.

Schelling, Thomas. 1963. *The Strategy of Conflict.* New York: Oxford University Press.

Silverstein, Lee. 1965. *Defense of the Poor in Criminal Cases in American State Courts.* American Bar Foundation.

Skinner, B.F. 1957. *Verbal Behavior.* New York: Appleton-Century-Crofts.

Skolnick, Jerome. 1967. Social Control in the Adversary System. *Journal of Conflict Resolution* 11:40.

Smith, Gerald W. 1970. *A Statistical Analysis of Public Defender Activities.* Columbus: Ohio State University Research Foundation.

_____, and Wendel, Max A. 1968. Public Defenders and Private Attorneys: A Comparison of Cases. *Legal Aid Briefcase* 27:95.

Southern California Law Review (Comment). 1969. Prosecutorial Discretion in the Initiation of Criminal Complaints. *Southern California Law Review* 42:519.

Spradley, James. 1970. *You Owe Yourself a Drunk.* Boston: Little, Brown.

_____, and McCurdy, David W. 1972. *The Cultural Experience: Ethnography in Complex Society.* Chicago: Science Research Associates.

Stover, Robert V., and Eckart, Dennis R. 1975. A Systematic Comparison of Public Defenders and Private Attorneys. *American Journal of Criminal Law* 3:265.

Subin, Harry I. 1966. *Criminal Justice in a Metropolitan Court.* Office of Criminal Justice, U.S. Department of Justice. Washington, D.C.: Government Printing Office.

Sudnow, David. 1965. Normal Crimes: Sociological Features of the Penal Code in a Public Defender Office. *Social Problems* 12:255.

Taylor, Jean G., and associates. 1972. An Analysis of Defense Counsel in the Processing of Felony Defendants in San Diego, California. *Denver Law Journal* 49:233.

_____. 1973. An Analysis of Defense Counsel in the Processing of Felony Defendants in Denver, Colorado. *Denver Law Journal* 50:9.

Tiffany, Lawrence, Avichai, Yakov, and Peters, Geoffrey W. 1975. A Statistical Analysis of Sentencing in Federal Courts: Defendants Convicted after Trial, 1967-1968. *Journal of Legal Studies* 4:369.

Trammell, George W. 1969. Control of System Policy and Practice by the Office of District Attorney in Brooklyn and Los Angeles. *Prosecutor* 5:242.

Trebach, A.S. 1964. *The Rationing of Justice.* New Brunswick: Rutgers University Press.

Tyler, Stephen A., ed. 1969. *Cognitive Anthropology.* New York: Holt, Rinehart, and Winston.

Uhlman, Thomas M. 1977. The Impact of Defendant Race in Trial-Court Sanctioning Decisions, in John A. Gardiner, ed. *Public Law and Public Policy.* New York: Praeger.

Utz, Pamela J. 1978. *Settling the Facts: Discretion and Negotiation in Criminal Court.* Lexington, Mass.: Lexington Books, D.C. Heath.

Vetri, Dominick R. 1964. Guilty Plea Bargaining: Compromises by Prosecutors to Secure Guilty Pleas. *University of Pennsylvania Law Review* 112:865.

Villasenor, Rudy. 1971. Downtown Jurors Will Be Selected from Entire County. *Los Angeles Times*, July 11, 1971, p. B.

White, Welsh. 1971. A Proposal for Reform of the Plea Bargaining Process. *University of Pennsylvania Law Review* 119:439.

Wildhorn, Sorrel, and associates. 1976. *Indicators of Justice: Measuring the Performance of Prosecution, Defense, and Court Agencies Involved in Felony Proceedings: Analysis and Demonstration.* Santa Monica: Rand Corporation.

Wilkerson, Glen. 1972. Public Defenders as Their Clients See Them. *American Journal of Criminal Law* 1:141.

Wood, Arthur Lewis. 1956. Informal Relations in the Practice of Criminal Law. *American Journal of Sociology* 62:48.

Wright, Eric. 1973. *The Politics of Punishment.* New York: Harper and Row.

Yale Law Journal. 1956. The Influence of the Defendant's Plea on Judicial Determination of Sentence. *Yale Law Journal* 66:204.

Zolin, Frank. 1969. *Executive Officer's Report 1968/1969.* Los Angeles: The Superior Court, Los Angeles County.

_____. 1971. *Executive Officer's Report 1970/1971.* Los Angeles: The Superior Court, Los Angeles County.

Index

Index

About the Author

Lynn M. Mather attended U.C.L.A. as an undergraduate, had graduate training in law and society at the University of California (Irvine and Berkeley), and received the Ph.D. in political science from the University of California, Irvine, in 1975. She was an instructor of political science at Grinnell College, Grinnell, Iowa, in 1971-72, and then began teaching at Dartmouth College, Hanover, New Hampshire, where she is currently an assistant professor of government. In 1977, Dr. Mather was a visiting assistant professor of political science at the University of California, San Diego. Dr. Mather is a member of the Board of Trustees of the Law and Society Association and has recently been awarded a grant to study trial courts, conflict, and conflict management.